`...the timber trees ...were the streightest, cleanest and I may say the larges

Northland, Kauri Forest

have ever seen … it was not one but all these trees which were enormous."
Bank's diary 30th March 1770

`` *The land has no rest, but is continually steep up and down , as if nature haa*

MacKenzie

"...etermined to try how much mountain she could place upon a given space."

Samuel Butler 1861

``Towards noon we saw a large high-lying land bearing south-east of us."

Golden Bay

Abel Tasman 13th December 1642

The·Birth·of
NEW ZEALAND
A Nation's Heritage

WARREN JACOBS

Text by John Wilson

Kowhai Publishing Limited

Acknowledgements

During the three and a half years that this book has been in the making, I have travelled the length and breadth of the country in all seasons searching out those subjects (sometimes obscure), that I could photograph to illustrate the birth of my homeland. All types of people assisted me in this from the directors of museums down to the young man who gave me a pillion ride on his motorcycle along the beach to the historic Kaipara lighthouse.

I wish to express my sincere thanks to all those people named and unnamed, the professionals and lay people alike, who helped with locating historical property and who provided the background information relating to the story. Also, I am indebted to the owners of private property and the curators and administrators of public property who showed so much enthusiasm and willingly allowed me access to their land.

Last but not least, I wish to thank my wife Sally for her help, encouragement and understanding, particularly during the formative months when we were struggling with the theme of the book.

W.J.

New Zealand Historic Places Trust
M. Trotter, J. Wilson, J. Queree,
R. Riccalton, A. Barker, G. Tunnicliffe
of the Canterbury Museum
Mr Fitzgerald, National Museum, Wellington
B. Skinner, Waitangi National Trust
Mr M. Stoddart, National Archive of
Department of Internal Affairs
Canterbury Provincial Buildings Board
I. Pentecost, Early Settlers Museum, Dunedin
Trounson Kauri Park
Hauraki Gulf Maritime Park
Russell Museum
Greytown Museum
Arrowtown Museum
Keri Keri model village
Goldfields Town, Queenstown
Shantytown, Greymouth
Mr Muir, Ferrymead, Christchurch
Christchurch Press Library
Wagner Museum, Hauhora Heads
Antigua Boatshed, Christchurch
Johnson & Couzins, Christchurch
G.H. Inwood, Rangiora
Emma Campbell, Christchurch
Adrienne Smith, Christchurch
Mr Jurlina, Sweetwater
Alex Bowman, Nelson
Rev. Reg Hall, Lyttelton
Mr & Mrs Val Currie, Mitchells Gully
Mr D. Thorpe, Alberton
Curator Larnach Castle
Curator Broadgreen, Nelson

P. O'Hagan, Highwic, Auckland
Curator Fyffe Cottage, Kaikoura
Curator Kemp House, Keri Keri
Aidan Challis, Waimate North Mission House
Curator Matanaka Otago
Omanaia Church parish
Pukehou Church parish
Dave Studholme, Te Waimate
Mr & Mrs Holden, Clendon House, Rawene
P. Nicholls, Pompallier House
Curator Melrose, Nelson
Curator Isel Park, Nelson
Curator Bishop School, Nelson
Curator Wylie Cottage, Gisborne
R. Cameron, Hayes Engineering Works
J. Webster, Ewelme Parnell
Curator Mangunga Mission House
Curator The Elms, Tauranga
Curator Hurworth, New Plymouth
Curator Matamata Tower
Mr & Mrs J. Howard, Westoe, Marton
Tom Gallagher, Oamaru
Galloway Station, Otago
Oruawharo, Hawkes Bay
Onoke, Hokianga Harbour
Woodstock, Stoke
McLeod family, Wantwood House, Mandeville
W. Thompson, Cottesbrook, Middlemarch
Morven Hills Station, Otago
Shag Valley Station, Otago
Beetham family, Brancepeth, Wairarapa
Coton Cottage committee, Horarata
Corwar Lodge committee

Published by Kowhai Publishing Ltd.
R.D. 1, Lyttelton
10 Peacock Street, Glendowie, Auckland
Reprinted 1995

Text set in 10pt Garamond type
Design and finished art by Nick Hawes and Judy Parker
Film positives made in Hong Kong
Printed and bound in China

To Sally

Contents

Aotearoa

" They have some arts among them which they execute with great judgement and unwearied patience."

James Cook 1773

Its Polynesian discoverers called it Aotearoa — the land of the long white cloud. Such a cloud, riding on the prevailing westerlies above New Zealand's mountain spine, told those first explorers of the Pacific, that land lay in the distant south-western corner of the world's largest ocean — two large fertile islands, hospitable to man, but the last of the world's major inhabitable areas to feel the tread of human feet.

The islands lay at the world's end, lost in their remote corner of the world's largest ocean, apart from human history. But men and women eventually found their way even to this last, furtherest corner of the world.

The occupation of New Zealand by Polynesians between about 750 and 1000 A.D. was the last step in a migration which began about 5000 B.C., when inhabitants of the peninsulas and islands of South East Asia began an extraordinary sea-borne expansion into the Indian and Pacific Oceans. They reached Fiji by about 1200 B.C., Tonga and Samoa by the time of Christ and the islands of Eastern Polynesia — the Cooks, the Marquesas, Tahiti — a few hundred years later. Between these islands and New Zealand lay 2500 kilometres of open ocean.

The ancestors of the Maori may have crossed this expanse of ocean by accident, drifting to these shores after being blown off course. Or they may, prompted by some sign of a distant land, perhaps the migratory flight of the shining cuckoo, have set out for New Zealand on a conscious voyage of discovery. The early Polynesians were skilled navigators and certainly did set out intent on finding new islands on which to settle, with plants and animals on board their double-hulled sailing canoes. New Zealand may have been discovered and occupied in this way. Perhaps both accidental drift and deliberate voyaging brought people to New Zealand from Eastern Polynesia during the era of Polynesian colonisation. Whether any early arrivals ever made return voyages to their home islands and persuaded others to return with them to New Zealand is another open question. Maori traditions suggest there were return voyages. These traditions tell of Kupe discovering land then returning to his home-land to give sailing instructions for the voyage to New Zealand. The traditions tell also of a grandfather, Whatonga, who set out to find a grandson, Toi, lost at sea and of the two eventually being reunited and settling in New Zealand which was already populated.

In their traditions, different Maori tribes trace their lines of descent back to ancestors who arrived in different canoes from their mythical homeland, Hawaiiki. These traditions were misinterpreted by the Europeans who first recorded them into the story that most of the early Maori arrived in a single fleet of seven canoes about 1350 A.D., displacing an earlier race, the Moriori.

But there was no Great Fleet and there were no New Zealanders before the ancestors of the Maori arrived here, intermittently, in small groups, over two or three hundred years. Some of the specific voyages mentioned in tribal traditions may refer to internal migrations as groups spread from initial landing points in New Zealand.

Behind the poetry of the traditions lies the fact that between about 750 and 800 A.D., Polynesian colonisers began to arrive in New Zealand from somewhere in East Polynesia until, probably about 1000 A.D., contact between New Zealand and the tropical islands from which the ancestors of the Maori came ceased.

Isolated in a large temperate country, the East Polynesian culture which these migrants brought to New Zealand evolved into the distinct Maori culture, one of the world's richest, most complex stone-age cultures. The Maori had a sophisticated knowledge of how to work different sorts of stone to provide tools or ornaments for different purposes. The objects they fashioned of greenstone, the most highly prized of all the stones, were of extraordinary beauty.

Using stone tools the Maori also carved wood and bone into objects of practical use and of exquisite beauty. Carving was a highly respected tapu occupation, and the works of the carvers, especially the great war canoes, were treasured possessions of the tribes. The Polynesians had arrived in New Zealand in double-hulled sailing canoes; by the time Europeans reached New Zealand most Maori canoes were single-hulled paddling canoes, better suited to fishing and coastal voyaging. Larger trees than are found on the islands were fashioned into magnificent carved vessels which aroused admiration in the first Europeans to see them.

The Maori also found in New Zealand, besides great trees, a plant, New Zealand flax, whose fibre they put to a great variety of uses. Of dressed flax the Maori wove fine cloaks and fashioned fishing nets, some of which were hundreds of metres long. The tough fibre was also fashioned into baskets — kits — used for carrying and storing foodstuffs and other items.

The large, forested country to which these first New Zealanders came provided many foods. The first arrivals lived as hunters and gatherers. From the sea they took fish and shellfish; from lakes and rivers they took eel; and from the forest, birds and berries. They harpooned seals and dolphins and dug for fernroot. The only animals they brought with them from the islands were the Polynesian dog and, possibly as a stowaway, the Polynesian rat. For a time, until hunting sealed the fate of a bird which had been declining in numbers because of environmental changes since the ice age, they had the flightless moa as a quarry. Moa were most plentiful in the eastern South Island and this region was the most heavily populated in the archaic or 'moa hunter' period of Maori culture.

The only crop which the Maori colonists brought with them from tropical Polynesia which flourished in colder New Zealand was the kumara, which had reached Polynesia from South America. Over the centuries the Maori learned how to grow and store kumara even where there were winter frosts. Gardens were protected by stone walls and soil was modified by adding sand, gravel or charcoal to give good crops. Large storage pits protected the crop through the winter.

Kumara could not be grown far south of Banks Peninsula and in southern New Zealand the Maori remained, until the time of European contact, predominantly hunters and gatherers. But elsewhere in New Zealand the spread of kumara cultivation was associated with marked cultural changes. The shift from the 'archaic' to the 'classical' periods of Maori culture did not occur uniformly throughout New Zealand over a short period of time. But by the time of European contact in the late 18th century, over much of the country the Maori were living rather different lives from those of the first arrivals nearly 1000 years earlier. They were settled gardeners rather than roving hunters and gatherers, although forest and sea continued to be important sources of food alongside the kumara gardens. The Maori of the classical period also ate enemies killed in battle and sometimes slaves killed for the purpose. Captain Cook found cannibalism hard to account for in a people 'naturally of a good disposition' whose 'behaviour to us was manly and mild, showing on all

occasions a readiness to oblige'. It is unlikely that the Maori ate human flesh primarily because food resources were inadequate. Rather it had become established as an ancient custom, of ritual significance and an utterly accepted part of the culture — the Maori merely laughed when the first Europeans and Polynesians who came with them expressed abhorrence of the practice.

Living relatively settled lives in their own tribal areas, the Maori of the classical period dotted the landscape with fortified villages — pa — often dramatically sited on headlands and ridge tops. The wooden and reed huts in which the inhabitants of the pa lived were protected by great palisades, ditches and ramparts. The construction of these pa were prodigious achievements when wooden scrapers and flax baskets for carrying earth were the only tools available. The Maori did not live all the time in fortified pa. There were unfortified kainga, groups of huts, by cultivations, at fishing grounds, wherever it was convenient to have more than temporary shelter. Most were, however, close enough to a pa that the inhabitants could take refuge if the tribe was attacked for warfare played an important part in pre-European Maori life.

Captain Cook decided they were living 'under perpetual apprehensions of being destroyed by each other'. Battles were fought, or raids mounted, as a result of disputes over women, the land, greenstone or food resources, but also over matters of tribal or personal honour; individuals and tribes were intensely jealous of their mana or standing and acutely sensitive to slights on their honour or ancestry. Pre-European Maori fighting was hand to hand. Personal bravery counted for much: the haka which proceeded battles were efforts to cow and intimidate opponents before the fighting began. Deception and subterfuge often carried the day. Though many died, the fighting was not as bloody as it became once the Maori had acquired muskets from the early Europeans.

The prevalence of fighting did not impede extensive trade between different tribal areas. Prized greenstone came from only a few locations in the South Island, but was fashioned by tribes throughout the country. Other useful types of stone found in restricted localities were traded far afield. Mutton birds, taken in great numbers on the islands in Foveaux Strait, were sent north in exchange for kumara and other products of warmer climes.

Socially, the Maori lived as a member of kin groups of different sizes. The whanau was an extended family group, the hapu or subtribe a grouping of whanau numbering possibly up to 500 persons, and the iwi or tribe a grouping of a number of hapu, all sharing descent from those who, by tradition, reached New Zealand in one canoe. The groups were all linked by kinship and traced their descent from common ancestors. The tribe's whakapapa or genealogy was remembered back to the first arrival in New Zealand. The focus of the communal lives of these groups was the marae, an open space within the pa or kainga where the community gathered for social or ritual occasions.

Within these groups there was a clear line of distinction between the families of chiefs and of commoners. The members of chiefly families enjoyed certain privileges, but life was general communal and democratic. Cook observed that "the head of each tribe, or family, seems to be respected; and their respect may, on some occasions, command obedience; but I doubt if any amongst them have either a right or a power to enforce it". Social control was achieved less by discipline and enforcement than by the voluntary acceptance of obligations to the kin group and by tapu — the belief that certain objects or activities were sacred and had to be treated with respect.

In tapu, the religion of the Maori meshed with their everyday life. From the myths and legends, songs and chants which have survived, we know that the Maori enjoyed a rich intellectual and spiritual life. They had their pantheon of gods — Rangi, Papa, their children Tane, Tu, Tangaroa and many others — and strong animist beliefs. The identity of a tribe was often linked to a mountain in the tribe's territory. All important activities, such as kumara planting, were surrounded by ritual observances. The Maori shared the mythological culture hero, Maui, with other Polynesian cultures. A rich vein of humour is evident in their stories of him.

Lacking a written language, the Maori displayed extraordinary feats of memory to pass on their knowledge and traditions — the genealogies, the karakia (incantations), waiata (songs and chants) in which the accumulated wisdom of the tribe was passed on to succeeding generations. A special group of men, tohunga, had spiritual powers; the group also included men with particular skills, the transmission of which was vital to the survival of the people.

The Maori people had a thousand years of history in New Zealand behind them by the late 18th century. In those thousand years the culture had changed, gently and slowly, reaching in some areas — the working of stone and carving of wood among them — greater heights than any other stone-age culture. The hundred years from the late 18th to the late 19th centuries were to see many of those achievements effaced for ever and the culture and people subjected to changes more rapid and far-reaching than they had known since the first Polynesians stepped ashore.

Maori carvers exercised their skill on a variety of materials including wood, stone and bone. A whalebone mere (fighting club) could be exquisitely decorated (Pg 15) with a carving of symbolic significance to the weapon's owner. Warfare was a constant feature of Maori life as tribe fought tribe over land or honour. Kapiti Island, (Pg. 16) bitterly fought over in the early nineteenth century became the stronghold of the Ngati Toa chief Te Rauparaha who dominated the Cook Strait area at the time of European settlement.

In pre-European times most Maori lived in simple huts, but on the tribe's important buildings — the meeting house, the dwellings of the rangatira (chiefs) and the pataka or storehouses where supplies of food were stored or tribal treasures kept safe — Maori carvers lavished their exceptional talents. A pataka such as this (Pg. 17) might have been carved over several generations.

The centre posts of substantial Maori buildings, which supported the ridgepole, were often carved as representations of tribal ancestors. (Left)

The carvings of a major tribal house could summarise a tribe's complete descent and history. The house itself was regarded as a personality in its own right.

While large, carved houses were built for communal purposes, the usual dwelling of most Maori in pre-European times was a low hut made of raupo reeds tied in bundles to a wooden frame. (Above Right)

From the trunks of forest giants, felled only after the proper incantations to Tane, the god of the forest, and following the strict rules of tapu, the Maori, using only stone adzes and fire, fashioned large, single-hulled canoes, decorated with elaborate carvings. These canoes, able to seat scores of warriors, were among the most treasured possessions of the tribes and excited the admiration of the first Europeans to see them on the New Zealand coast. (Top Left)

The Maori of classic times was a gardener, growing kumara in carefully tended gardens, but the sea remained a major source of food. Fish were caught on hook and line or in huge nets woven of flax. Kina (sea eggs) and mussels (Above) were collected off reefs. Productive reefs were the jealously protected preserves of the tribes owning them.

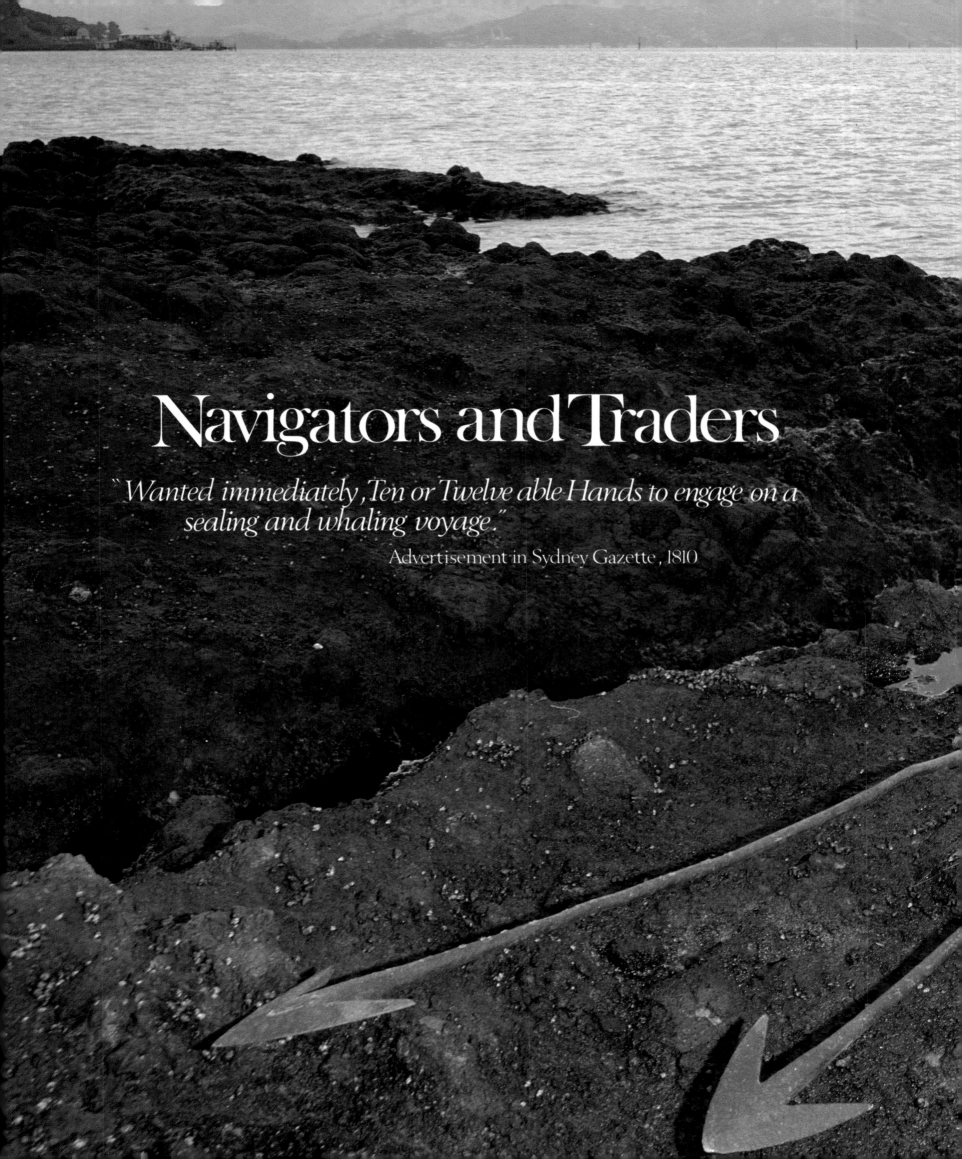

Navigators and Traders

"Wanted immediately, Ten or Twelve able Hands to engage on a sealing and whaling voyage."

Advertisement in Sydney Gazette, 1810

In 1642 Abel Tasman sailed from Batavia (now Jakarta) in the Dutch East Indies (now Indonesia) to discover the great southern continent which many Europeans believed must lie in the far reaches of the southern ocean, not yet traversed by European ships. On the 13th December 1642 Tasman sighted land, not the sought-after southern continent but the high ranges behind the western coast of the South Island of New Zealand.

Tasman sailed north up the coast and on the 18th December anchored in a bay "by him called Murderers Bay, by reason of some of his men being killed by the natives". The unfortunate affray — in which four Dutchmen were killed — and his belief that the inhospitable land he had discovered offered no prospect of treasure prompted Tasman, after sailing north to the tip of the North Island, to quit the land named soon after by other Dutchmen, 'Nieuw Zeeland'.

Tasman left on the map a tantalising line which many in Europe confidently believed was the western coast of the great southern continent. 130 years later the greatest of the Pacific navigators, James Cook, showed that Tasman's inconclusive line was the western coast, not of a continent, but of two large, inhabited islands.

Cook, in command of a converted collier, the Endeavour, was despatched from England in 1769, first to observe the transit of Venus at Tahiti in June 1769 then to sail south to look for the supposed southern continent and then, if that search were unsuccessful, east to investigate Tasman's New Zealand.

In October 1769, from the masthead of the Endeavour, a cabin boy, Nicholas Young, sighted land. On the 9th Cook, having brought the Endeavour to anchor in Poverty Bay, became the first European to land on New Zealand soil. Cook remained in New Zealand waters on this first voyage until April 1770. He circumnavigated both islands, dispelling forever the notion that Tasman's New Zealand was part of a southern continent. (Some on board the Endeavour persisted in believing that it might be, until at the bottom of the South Island a swell from the south convinced them that the South Island could not be a great promontory attached to a southern continent). On his first visit Cook laid down New Zealand's coastline on charts more accurately than any first explorer of any other new land.

Cook returned to New Zealand on both his second and third voyages to the Pacific in the 1770s. He used New Zealand harbours — especially Ship Cove in the Marlborough Sounds and Dusky Sound in the far south-west — as places of rest and refreshment during his restless probing of the Pacific. Cook left a perceptive and detailed description of New Zealand and its inhabitants as a result of these visits. He described the country as a land often "rude and craggy", hilly, well-covered with woods and well inhabited, especially the North Island.

There were occasional clashes between Maori and men of Cook's parties, but at other times there were amicable and intrigued encounters between Maori and European. Cook formed a high opinion of the race, notwithstanding his discovery that they were cannibals. He accurately anticipated New Zealand's future when he recorded, on his first voyage, the general opinion aboard the Endeavour that "was this country settled by an industrious people, they would very soon be supplied not only with the necessaries but many of the luxuries of life".

After Tasman, New Zealand and its Maori inhabitants had been left alone again for more than a century. It was very different after Cook. The first on his heels were other navigators and discoverers — the French navigator de Surville was briefly in New Zealand waters at the time of Cook's first voyage and only a storm as they each rounded the northern tip of the North Island prevented what would have been an unexpected meeting in remote seas. Another Frenchman, Marion du Fresne, visited New Zealand in 1772, to be killed with more than a score of his men in the Bay of Islands. Vancouver, D'Entrecastaux, Malaspina and D'Urville all contributed to the further exploration and charting of the long coastline of New Zealand.

Cook had observed in New Zealand excellent timber for ships' masts and "a kind of very broad bladed grass" (flax) from which, he concluded, observing that the Maori used it to make baskets, mats and nets; it would be possible to make rope and canvas. Cook's Journal, published in 1777, helped to arouse interest in these and other New Zealand resources. The first cargo of spars was collected from New Zealand's vast native forests in the mid 1790s. (The kauri tree, which gave the best of these spars, also exuded a resin which, when fossilised, became kauri gum. The first cargo of gum was exported from New Zealand in 1815). For cargoes of flax, the early traders to New Zealand relied on the Maori to dress the fibre. In their eagerness to acquire European goods, especially guns but also cloth and iron nails, Maori tribes dressed tons of flax to barter with the traders.

But it was products of the sea rather than the land which brought Europeans in greater numbers to live in, rather than visit, New Zealand. In the early 1790s, sealing gangs were landed on the southern coasts. So thorough was the slaughter of seals by these gangs, who lived rough and precarious lives ashore, that by the end of the first decade of the nineteenth century the trade in seal skins was already declining. About the same time, sperm whalers began to frequent New Zealand waters, putting, in increasing numbers after about 1800, into the Bay of Islands. There they traded blankets, knives and guns for potatoes, pork and the favours of Maori women.

Around 1830, the whaling industry took a new turn. The quarry became the southern right or black whale taken not from whaling ships but from shore stations. Small, rough European settlements sprang up on the shores of Foveaux and Cook Straits, up the East Coast of the South Island and at one or two places further north.

About the same time some flax and other traders ceased to move on ships from harbour to harbour searching out cargoes, choosing rather to settle ashore to assemble cargoes for loading when the ships returned. Many of these early resident traders and whalers took Maori women as their wives. Some became Pakeha-Maori, adopting many of the customs and ways of life of the race which still dominated New Zealand. The Bay of Islands remained the most important refitting point and centre of general trade between Maori and European. Kororareka (now Russell) became, about 1830, New Zealand's first proper European town.

Long before organised settlement began in the 1840s, New Zealand was already home to several hundred Europeans. The European population of New Zealand in 1830 was probably a little more than 300. By 1839 the number had risen to possibly 2000. They were a handful measured against the numbers of Maori and were largely confined to the coasts. But their impact on Maori society was devastating. This was not because there were frequent clashes between Maori and Pakeha in the early years of the nineteenth century. There were a few ugly incidents, like the Boyd 'massacre' of 1809, when a body of Maori attacked a European ship and Europeans later retaliated savagely, but on the whole there was relatively little conflict between Maori and European in this era, when members of each race were supplying members of the other with goods the other wanted.

But what many Maori sought most eagerly were muskets to turn not against Europeans but against other Maori. The introduction of guns into Maori tribal warfare led to fighting far more lethal than fighting using only traditional weapons. In the 1820s Hongi Hika led the Nga Puhi of Northland, one of the first tribes to acquire good numbers of muskets, south to lay waste the territory of other tribes. A little later, further south, Te Rauparaha fought to establish his tribe, Ngati Toa, on Kapiti Island and the nearby coast of the North Island, then carried war to the Ngai Tahu of the South Island. Thousands died in these and other tribal conflicts.

Besides guns, the first Europeans brought to New Zealand other things of deadly impact on the Maori — new diseases and alcohol. Epidemics raged among the Maori who lacked resistance to new diseases. Thousands more died, even in communities far from direct contact with any Europeans. Alcohol also had destructive effects on Maori life. Under these combined stresses, the Maori population seems to have declined significantly. By 1840 there were probably just over 100,000 Maori in New Zealand. 70 years earlier, when Cook's arrival ushered in the age of European impact on New Zealand, there were probably at least twice but possibly four times this number. A large part of the Maori population remained remote from any direct contact with Europeans and the impact of musket warfare and disease was less severe in some places than in others. But the impact of the arrival of Europeans on the Maori was, if not 'fatal', certainly very damaging.

The generation of tribal warfare, fought with muskets, ended about the mid 1830s, partly because the warring tribes had exhausted themselves. But some credit for the end of the fighting must go to a group of Europeans who came to New Zealand not to make their own fortunes (although some later did) but for higher, unselfish motives.

Many of the earliest Pakeha New Zealanders were rough, wild men, runaway convicts and the riff-raff of several nationalities. To other Europeans they appeared "a most worthless class of persons...keepers of grog shops, and other vagabonds of dissolute habits" who encouraged the natural vices of the natives and taught them new ones. But also among the earliest Europeans to settle permanently in New Zealand were the missionaries.

Many of the goods exported from New Zealand in these early years of European contact — flax, timber, whale oil, whale bone and foodstuffs — found their way to Sydney. New Zealand was drawn into the world of European commerce by Australian expansion. And from Australia too flowed the impulse to bring the benefits of Christianity and European civilisation to the Maori.

Compass, chronometer and telescope helped James Cook to rediscover New Zealand in the eighteenth century and to make an astonishingly accurate chart of its coastline. Among the effects in his cabin (Below) were also the quill pens which he used to write the Journals which gave Europe a vivid first impression of the strange and remote islands he explored.

Cook brought New Zealand into the awareness of Europe at the height of the Age of Enlightenment, when European curiosity about the natural world was high. With Cook on his voyages were scientists and naturalists who were avid collectors of the strange new plants and animals they encountered on the islands of New Zealand. (Opp. Below Left)

New Zealand's sheltered harbours and bays provided the early navigators, and the sealers, whalers and traders who soon followed them, with safe anchorages and opportunities to take on water and other supplies. Soon after he first reached New Zealand in 1769, Cook found a cove in Tolaga Bay (Opp. Top) where he was able to take on wood and water to replenish the Endeavour after the voyage from Tahiti.

Cook and his fellow explorers had scarcely charted the New Zealand coastline when small trading vessels, (Inset Pg 22) most of them based at the newly founded settlement of Sydney, began to frequent New Zealand waters. They came seeking cargoes of timber and flax, often supplied by Maori keen to secure European goods from across the Tasman Sea.

ENDEAVOUR

Among the products sought by the earliest Europeans to exploit the natural riches of New Zealand were seal skins, whale oil, whalebone and dressed flax. Large colonies of the southern fur seal (Far Left) on New Zealand's southern coasts were reduced in a few years to remnants by greedy sealing gangs. The blubber of beached whales, dragged ashore at the shore whaling stations established in the 1830s, was reduced to oil in iron trypots (Left) which have outlasted the crude sheds and shacks of the stations. Maori tribes, anxious to secure nails, blankets, tobacco and above all muskets from Sydney-based traders, dressed the long, tough leaves of native flax plant, harakeke, (Bottom Left) into a strong fibre from which rope was made.

Many shore whaling stations were abandoned after a few years, the rough dwellings and simple equipment mostly soon vanishing. Other stations survived to become coastal farming and fishing settlements. At Matanaka, on the Otago coast, John Jones transformed a shore whaling station which he bought in 1838 into a thriving agricultural community, some years before the main body of settlers arrived in Otago. Jones built farm buildings (Overleaf) to serve the farm which he established on a headland above the whaling station. The largest of the buildings was a fine stable (Below) built to house the horses which he brought over from Sydney to work the farm. At Kaikoura, further north on the South Island's east coast, George Fyffe, about 1860, built a house (Opp. Middle) for himself and his bride at the Waiopuka whaling station which his cousin, Robert Fyffe, had established in 1843. The Fyffes ran sheep and goats on a nearby run as well as catching whales and from their Waiopuka station grew the town of Kaikoura.

Missionaries and Explorers

"Behold I bring you good tidings of great joy."
Samuel Marsden   Christmas Day 1814

A bluff, practical man, Samuel Marsden was a prison chaplain in Sydney, whose interest in New Zealand was aroused by encounters with occasional Maori who turned up in Sydney as seamen on whaling and trading vessels. Marsden eventually prevailed on the authorities in New South Wales to allow him to carry the gospel across the Tasman. On Christmas Day, 1814, he landed in the Bay of Islands and preached a sermon on the text ''Behold I bring you good tidings of great joy''.

Marsden believed it was his duty to take to the Maori the benefits not only of the Christian religion but also of European civilisation. He therefore sent to New Zealand over the next few years from his base in New South Wales men who could not only preach the gospel but also teach the arts and skills of Europe to the natives.

He founded New Zealand's first mission station on his first visit in 1814. On return visits in later years he founded further stations in Northland, bringing with him on a visit in 1823 a young missionary, Henry Williams, under whose energetic and able leadership the Anglican mission flourished and expanded after early difficult years.

The first Wesleyan missionaries arrived in New Zealand in 1822. After initial difficulties of their own, they became strongly entrenched in Northland. The arrival of a French bishop, Pompallier, in 1838 saw the beginning of Roman Catholic mission work. By 1840 there were mission stations far to the south of the Bay of Islands, at Kawhia, in the Bay of Plenty, on the Kapiti Coast and inland, in the Waikato and Waipa Valleys. The missionaries at first made scant impression on the beliefs of the Maori. In 1825 Henry Williams complained that the natives were ''as insensible to the necessity of redemption as brutes''

The author of the first history of New Zealand, published in 1858, described the missionaries as, for 15 years, ''men crying in the wilderness''. Some missionaries likened their work to casting seed on a rock. But after about 1830 the scattered seed began, at last to sprout. This was the result, in part, of the work not of European missionaries but of Maori evangelists who, converted and trained at one of the mission stations, went ahead of the missionaries themselves carrying the gospel to more remote tribes. As increasing numbers of Maori were converted to Christianity tribal warfare, and cannibalism, virtually ceased. Captives were released to return to their own tribes.

As Marsden had intended when he launched his mission to the Maori, the missionaries brought not only Christianity but also literacy and a knowledge of European crafts and farming techniques. The Church Missionary Society sympathised with Marsden's conviction that the Maori had to be civilised as well as converted and sent out farmers and artisans as well as men of the cloth to its mission stations.

At Waimate North, the country's first inland mission station, New Zealand's first European style farm was established in the 1830s. There Maori converts learned how to grow European crops, mill wheat and other new skills. Flourishing Maori agricultural communities in the Waikato and the Firth of Thames grew agricultural products for export to Australia and in the 1840s supplied the struggling young European settlements with foodstuffs. Some Maori moved, within one lifetime, from the stone to the iron age and from supplementing the cultivation of one staple crop, the kumara, with fishing and hunting to being sedentary and prosperous farmers growing a number of crops. The missionaries brought much more than the Christian religion to the people they had come to convert.

New Zealand's first missionary — Samuel Marsden — was also one of New Zealand's first inland explorers. Although already in his fifties, he made arduous journeys on his first and subsequent visits which helped to establish the lie of the land from the Firth of Thames north to the Bay of Islands for other Europeans. Through the 1830s and 1840s other missionaries undertook some of the great journeys of North Island exploration. William Colenso, for one, explored the Ruahine Range of inland Hawkes Bay.

When European settlers began to arrive in significant numbers, the country's few clergy had to travel widely to minister to their flocks. Their journeys added a further clerical contribution to the exploration of New Zealand. Few clergymen travelled more widely than Bishop Selwyn, who arrived in New Zealand in 1842. Several of Bishop Selwyn's 'visitation tours' took on, at least in part, the character of exploratory expeditions. In the South Island, Bishop Harper of Canterbury made comparable journeys in the 1850s while tending to his scattered flock.

But not all the early explorers were missionaries or clergymen. The greatest epic of New Zealand exploration was the expedition in the late 1840s of Thomas Brunner from Nelson down the Buller River and the West Coast of the South Island as far as Paringa, a return journey which took 550 days. What impelled Brunner to endure the privations of his journey (he was once so short of food he was obliged to eat his dog) was the pleasure of traversing new country and the joy of discovering new routes and new resources. He had no wish or expectation to profit personally from his discoveries.

Other explorers were driven by motives of gain. The writer Samuel Butler, who spent four years in the early 1860s in Canterbury, felt the urge to explore new country for the sake of exploration alone — ''As soon as I saw the mountains'' he wrote, ''I longed to get on the other side of them'' — but the main purpose of his journeys in the early 1860s to the headwaters of the Waimakariri, Rakaia and Rangitata Rivers in Canterbury was to find unoccupied 'country' on which he could run sheep. Some early gold prospectors and miners became explorers inadvertently in their pursuit of gold.

Some exploration was undertaken by Government employees. Surveyors such as John Thompson, who explored Central Otago and the Waitaki Valley, and scientists and naturalists like Julius Haast and James Hector, the Provincial Geologists of Canterbury and Otago, were drawn into remote parts of the country by the prospect of discovering new forms of plant or bird life or of attaining a better understanding of the country's geological structure. (The politicians who employed them hoped they might find payable mineral deposits). Earlier, a naturalist, Ernst Dieffenbach, had been the first European to climb Taranaki (Mount Egmont) and to penetrate the Central North Island plateau and thermal regions.

Yet another motive for journeys of exploration was the wish to find feasible overland routes between the isolated early settlements. Parts of the northern part of the South Island were first explored by men seeking routes to bring stock from Nelson and Marlborough into Canterbury.

Many of the early European explorers of New Zealand were led by Maori guides and followed ancient Maori tracks. These tracks crossed even the perilous ranges of the Southern Alps, through which the Maori had found the passes over which they brought greenstone from Westland into Canterbury. Brunner, whose name stands highest in the annals of New Zealand exploration, had with him a ''faithful and attached servant'' E. Kehu who was "worth his weight in tobacco" for his abilities to manage a canoe, snare wild fowl, ford a river and shoot. Much credit is due to the early European explorers who gradually pieced together the inland topography of New Zealand, but the Maori before them had been familiar with every corner of New Zealand and many journeys of European exploration were only successful because the explorers could draw on Maori knowledge of the country and Maori skill at surviving in it.

Some parts of New Zealand, especially the open plains and valleys of parts of the South Island, were easy going for early travellers. But the South Island also had more massive mountains and swifter more turbulent rivers than the North which made it more difficult to traverse. "The land has no rest" Butler complained "but is continually steep up and down, as if nature had determined to try how much mountain she could place upon a given space." The tangled, heavily bushed ranges of the North Island were lower than the South Island's mountains, but posed problems and challenges of their own to explorers. It was not until the 1890s, three-quarters of a century after the missionaries, seeking further souls to save, first began to explore beyond the coast that all the main features of New Zealand were mapped. Even then there remained odd corners of country unexplored and the last paragraphs of the story of New Zealand exploration were not written until the 1930s.

On Christmas Day, 1814, New Zealand's first missionary, Samuel
Marsden, came ashore at Oihi on the northern side of the Bay of Islands
and proclaimed the Christian gospel in New Zealand. There was then a
pa nearby, but the now deserted site is marked only by a stone cross.
(Inset Pg. 32)

The first missionaries came to a wild, primitive country, but were quick
to build for themselves substantial houses in which they could lead the
decent, civilised and Christian lives to which they hoped to convert the
'savages' of New Zealand. The Kemp House, Kerikeri (Above) was built
in 1821-22 for the supervisor of the second mission station which
Marsden established, near an important Maori settlement, in 1819.
Marsden staffed his mission stations with practical men, artisans and
farmers as well as clergymen missionaries. The missionaries themselves
were men of culture and learning and brought with them the desks (Far
Left) and books they needed to be able to continue to cultivate their
minds in a rough and to them semi-barbarous land.

The mission stations had to be kept supplied with goods from Sydney —
rice, sugar, salt and other rations for the mission families, blankets and
tobacco for trade with the local Maori, axes and hoes for the mission
gardens, slates and pencils for the mission schools, nails and saws for
the erection of mission buildings. Between 1832 and 1836 a large stone
store house was built at Kerikeri (Left), partly of local stone and partly
of sandstone brought over from Sydney, to keep the mission's many
supplies safe. When Bishop Selwyn arrived in New Zealand in the
early 1840s, he was glad to find a building in which he could keep his
precious library safe from fire.

For several years the missionaries lived in stations on the coast, only occasionally venturing inland. In 1830, Marsden fulfilled a long-standing ambition and established a mission station at Waimate North, 15 kilometres inland from the Bay of Islands. Three mission houses were built in 1831-32 by Maori carpenters working under missionary supervision.

Local kauri was used for the buildings. New Zealand's first European farm was established by the missionaries at Waimate North. Farm buildings and a mill were erected and within a few years Waimate North was a thriving agricultural settlement. Maori and Pakeha worked side by side growing fruit, grain and vegetables and tending pigs and poultry. Maori children were being taught in the mission school.

After building the houses, stores and other buildings needed to meet their immediate, practical requirements, the missionaries were quick to erect chapels and then larger churches in which they, and they hoped their converts, could worship. The first chapel at Waimate North was built soon after the founding of the station. The present Church of St John the Baptist (Far Left) was not built until 1870-71, but it incorporates timber and furnishings from the second chapel which it replaced.

After Bishop Selwyn arrived in New Zealand in 1842, he leased the Waimate mission station from the Church Missionary Society. The Waimate Mission House became his 'palace'. Mrs Selwyn found the interior of the house (Below & Left) somewhat dismal and inconvenient and made a number of internal changes and had it painted to make it more liveable and cheerful. But it remained a simple house, if well-furbished for the time.

The kitchen of the Waimate Mission House (Overleaf) is lined with the original finely adzed wide kauri boards. Into the kitchen projects the fireplace and oven which were built originally of bricks handmade on the site.

Though they were built in New Zealand when the country was still rough and wild, the joinery of the early mission houses (Below Right) was careful and exact, the motif of the cross reflecting the reason the missionaries ventured to New Zealand at all.

Stout wooden chests brought the personal possessions of missionaries and other settlers to New Zealand. (Above) Anglicans were soon followed by Methodists as missionaries to the Maori. One of the Methodists' main fields was the Hokianga. At Mangungu they built a mission house (Pg 42 Lower Right) to replace an earlier house which burned down in 1838.

When Bishop Pompallier, a Frenchman, established his Roman Catholic mission at Kororareka (now Russell) in 1839, one of the first buildings erected was a solid structure of packed earth and timber (Pg 43 Lower Right) to house the mission's printing press

(Pg 42 Bottom) From this and other mission presses flowed the first books in Maori which helped to spread Christianity and literacy among tribes remote from the missionaries' direct influence.

In 1835 a chapel, now Christ Church, Russell (Pg 43 Lower Left) was built at Kororareka, then a rollicking trading town, in need, the missionaries felt, of Christian influence.

From their foothold in the North, the missionaries gradually extended their work south. A mission house, now known as The Elms, (Pg 43 Centre) was built in 1847 at the Te Papa mission station which had been founded at Tauranga in 1835.

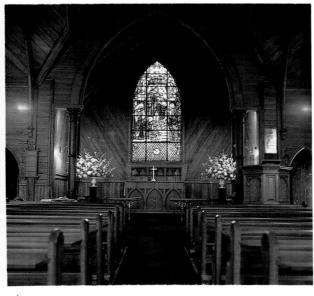

After years of holding fast to their own beliefs, many Maori from the mid 1830s embraced Christianity. In the unique wooden headboards of the Hokianga (Opp. Top Left) Christian elements blend with traditional Maori motifs. Many Maori accepted Christianity without abandoning completely their own culture.

By the 1850s, missionaries were active throughout the country, evangelising and educating the Maori. Christ Church, Pukehou, (Left and Opp. Top Right) the oldest in Hawkes Bay, was built about 1858, near a college which the missionaries had founded a few years earlier for the education of Maori boys.

43

Victoria by the Grace of God of the United Kingdom of Great Britain and Ireland Queen Defender of the Faith To our trusty and welbeloved John Hobson ... **Whereas** by an Act of Parliament intituled – "An Act to continue in force ... of Parliament and ... an Act of Parliament made and passed in the ... Reign intituled ... thousand eight hundred and forty one ... for the administration of Justice in New South ... for the more effectual Government the ... amongst other things) enacted that ... to be from time to time ... to erect ... into a separate ... hereafter may be conta... New South Wales ... in Us vested in and ... certain Letters Patent Ireland ... Britain and ... New Zealand and ... in the South year ... New South

Ruling a New Colony

"Oh Governor, stay. Do not go away from us, remain for us a father, a judge, a peacemaker....Sit here, dwell in our midst."

Tamati Waka Nene   5th February 1840

In 1840 New Zealand became a British colony. It was the most important single event in the country's story since the first Polynesians landed, at least a thousand years before. New Zealand's links with Great Britain became close in the following century, but in the late 1830s a reluctant British Government dragged its feet over bringing New Zealand into the Empire as a new colony.

The debate in Britain over whether Britain should annex New Zealand was sparked by mounting lawlessness and violence in New Zealand itself. One visitor of 1839 concluded that the Bay of Islands contained "a greater number of rogues than any other spot of equal size in the universe". Some Europeans in New Zealand were undoubtedly rough and unprincipled, not quite "the veriest refuse of civilised society" as one minister in New South Wales described them, but unruly and lawless.

The solid and respectable members of the European community in New Zealand — some traders and the missionaries — appalled by the behaviour of other Europeans in the country, petitioned the British Government to do something about the situation in New Zealand and the Bay of Islands in particular.

In the 1830s the Governments of New South Wales and of the United Kingdom felt obliged to take some steps — short of annexation at first — to protect British subjects against the attacks by Maori and lawless Europeans, and also to protect the Maori against the exploitation and brutality of those same lawless Europeans. In 1833 the British Government took a first step and sent James Busby across from Sydney to act as British Resident in New Zealand. He was charged with keeping law and order, helping law-abiding settlers, encouraging trade and returning escaped convicts. Busby has gone down in history as "a man without guns". A pompous, self-important young man, he was put in a situation in which even a stronger more effective character would have been unable to do much. Reluctant to become too responsible for what was happening in New Zealand, the British Government gave Busby neither real authority nor troops. The appointment was the least the British Government felt it could get away with without being charged with neglecting British interests.

After Busby had arrived in the Bay of Islands 'Baron' Charles de Thierry appeared on the scene with pretensions of establishing himself as a ruler. de Thierry's arrival prompted Busby to induce 35 Maori chiefs to sign a Declaration of Independence, which was scornfully dismissed at the time as a "paper pellet fired off at de Thierry". Paper pellet it may have been, but the declaration embodied an important principle which became the basis of British policy in New Zealand — that the Maori chiefs were sovereign in New Zealand and the Maori people the owners of the country.

The notion that the aboriginal inhabitants had rights to New Zealand which prevented Britain or any other power from simply walking in and taking the country over had been expressed many decades earlier. The President of the Royal Society had told Cook that "no European nation has a right to occupy any part of their country or settle among them without their voluntary consent". The principle on which Busby acted in attempting to thwart de Thierry — that the Maori chiefs were sovereigns whose consent would be needed before New Zealand could be annexed — dictated that in 1840, after the British Government had finally decided to act, William Hobson, sent to annex New Zealand, would set out to sign a treaty with the independent native chiefs before proclaiming British sovereignty.

In the late 1830s the British Government came under conflicting pressures as the debate whether Britain should annex New Zealand became more vigorous. The prime concern of the missionaries and humanitarians was to protect the Maori from exploitation and oppression by large numbers of European settlers until the Maori had been converted and civilised and were able to hold their own. Those on this side of the debate differed among themselves whether this meant European settlement should be totally prohibited or merely subject to strict controls, but their shared concern was that unchecked European colonisation could be a calamity for the Maori.

But at the same time interest in New Zealand as a country suitable for settlement by large numbers of Europeans was growing in Britain. Those who espoused the cause of settlement wanted Britain to assert its authority in New Zealand so that the country could be colonised by Europeans in an orderly manner.

The British Government took a middle path between these conflicting views. It accepted, realistically, that colonisation could not be prevented, but was anxious also to protect the Maori people from subjugation or extermination in any "process of war and spoliation" — which had already been the fate of other native peoples in lands settled by Europeans. The British Colonial Office sought to avert "the evils...resulting from irregular and lawless colonisation" without preventing settlement entirely. By the late 1830s the British Government was reconciled to annexing New Zealand as the only way in which the interests of both the Maori and prospective settlers could be balanced.

Partisans of the New Zealand Company — set up to promote European settlement in New Zealand — liked to suggest that the British Government decided to annex New Zealand only after the Company had forced the Government's hand by despatching the Tory to New Zealand in May 1893 to purchase land on which it could plant a settlement. In fact the Company despatched the Tory abruptly because it anticipated, correctly, that the Government was about to act and would, in the interests of protecting the Maori from exploitation, take control of the acquisition of land from the Maori, making it difficult if not impossible for the Company to buy land itself from individual chiefs or tribes. At the most, the Company's action in despatching the Tory merely forced the British Government to act faster than it might otherwise have acted and made Lieutenant-Governor Hobson waste no time, when he arrived in New Zealand early in 1840, in securing the consent of the Maori chiefs to British annexation.

In August 1839 Hobson, a naval captain who had visited New Zealand in 1837, was instructed to proceed to New Zealand to negotiate with the Maori to get them to recognise the sovereignty of Queen Victoria in return for a guarantee of their rights to ownership of the land. The Maoris, Hobson was told, were "a numerous and inoffensive people, whose title to the soil and the sovereignty of New Zealand is indisputable". He was ordered to obtain their "free and intelligent consent" to British annexation of New Zealand.

Within a week of arriving in the Bay of Islands on January 29 1840 Hobson had assembled a number of Northland Maori at Waitangi, where Busby had his residence. The crowd which gathered there on February 5 was large and colourful: Hobson in his full dress uniform, the Anglican clergy and Catholic bishop, a knot of local settlers, the many chiefs, some in fine cloaks, others wearing blankets. A spirited debate began. Some of the chiefs voiced their fears for the future of their race in a New Zealand dominated by Europeans. New Zealand's future hung in the balance, for had a majority of the Maori chiefs refused to accept him and sign the treaty he had drawn up, with missionary help, Hobson could not, obedient to his instructions, have annexed New Zealand. The balance was swung in part by Tamati Waka Nene: "Remain with us" he told Hobson "a father, a judge, a peacemaker. You must not allow us to become slaves. You must preserve our customs and never permit our lands to be wrested from us".

On February 6 some 50 chiefs signed the treaty. Over the next few months copies of it were carried around New Zealand and about 500 more chiefs signed, although the signatories by no means represented all the tribes of New Zealand. After May 21 this became a somewhat academic point, for on that day Hobson proclaimed British sovereignty over the whole country — by right of discovery in the case of the South Island, by right of cession in the case of the North. New Zealand had become a British possession.

The treaty which provided justification for Hobson's annexation of New Zealand is regarded as the founding document of the New Zealand nation, although its legal standing is dubious and many New Zealanders question whether it has been properly observed. There were discrepancies between the document translated into Maori which the chiefs signed and the original text in English which suggest to some a deliberate attempt to conceal from the assembled chiefs the true import of the document they were being asked to sign. Under the treaty, in its English version, the chiefs ceded their sovereignty to the British Crown (with most probably not fully appreciating what the word meant), gaining in return 'all the rights and privileges of British subjects' and the 'full exclusive and undisturbed possession' of their lands, forests and fisheries. They could sell their land only to the Crown — strictly an infringement on their rights as British subjects, but one intended to be for their benefit.

Once the treaty had been signed at Waitangi Hobson declared, with satisfaction but also with excessive optimism, that "we are now one people". The treaty cleared the way for the annexation of New Zealand by Britain, but it also sowed seeds of future misunderstanding and discord. Even Tamati Waka Nene's endorsement of the treaty implied there were conditions on which the chiefs accepted Hobson, and when significant numbers of Maori ceased to believe that a later Governor was acting as Tamati Waka Nene enjoined Hobson to act, war resulted.

Probably very few of the chiefs anticipated how many Europeans were soon to come flooding into New Zealand. For some Maoris the disillusionment with the compact entered into at Waitangi in February 1840 came swiftly. "The shadow of the land" said the chief Nopera Panakaraeo in May 1840 "goes to Queen Victoria, but the substance remains to us". Less than a year later, in January 1841, he amended his remark: "the substance of the land goes to the Europeans, the shadow only will be our portion".

But whatever doubt can be cast on the motives of some British in securing the consent of the Maori to the treaty and however imperfectly its provisions have been honoured, the treaty did embody a principle crucial to the future development of New Zealand: that the country had belonged originally to its native inhabitants and that the two races had equal standing in it.

On annexation, New Zealand became a dependency of New South Wales, but this dependence was short-lived. In May 1841 New Zealand was proclaimed a Crown Colony in its own right. In January 1841 Hobson had shifted the seat of Government from Kororareka (Russell) to Auckland (where it remained until 1865). Hobson died in office in 1842 and was succeeded as

Governor by Robert FitzRoy, who was succeeded in turn in 1845 by one of the giants of New Zealand's early years, George Grey.

Over the next decade, acts of the British Parliament gave New Zealand the constitutions under which it was to be governed. The first of these was the 1846 Constitution Act, which conferred representative government on New Zealand by providing for an assembly elected by the settlers. On Grey's request, the bringing into force of this act was postponed. Although a democrat by conviction, Grey hesitated to yield any of his powers as Governor to an elected assembly in part because he feared European popular rule would jeopardise the interests of the Maori and excite their hostility. He feared also that large landowners would dominate the assembly to the disadvantage of the small farmers, of whose interests he was the ardent champion.

In 1852 the British Parliament passed a further New Zealand Constitution Act. This divided New Zealand into six provinces, each with their own Provincial Council and Superintendent. The act also established a central Government with an elected House of Representatives and an appointed Legislative Council or Upper House. Ownership of a small amount of property qualified men for the vote. Although plural voting allowed men of more property to dominate elections, New Zealand had a democratic form of government — by the standards of the day — only a dozen years after European settlers began to arrive in any numbers.

When the 1852 Constitution came into effect in 1853, Grey bowed out as Governor. It was left to the Administrator who filled the office of Governor between Grey's departure at the end of 1853 and the arrival of his successor, Thomas Gore Browne, in September 1855 to attempt to resist the demand that ministers — the Governor's advisers — should have seats in the House of Representatives and be able to command the support of a majority in the House. This demand — in effect a demand for complete self-government by the settlers — was voiced as soon as the General Assembly first met in 1854. Early in 1855 the Administrator was told by the Colonial Office that he should accede to the settlers' demands for "Government by the Leaders of the Parliamentary majority", 'reserving' to the Governor only control of Maori affairs and so, importantly, control of the purchase of land from the Maori. So New Zealanders were in effect given, without struggle or conflict, the right to govern themselves for which other peoples have been forced to fight. The other possible source of tension in the Constitution of 1852 was between the provincial and central Governments. The Constitution gave the provinces considerable powers over such matters as immigration, education and public works without specifying precisely which branch of government was to expend revenues raised. An agreement — 'the Compact of 1856' — was hammered out to resolve this tension.

Although there were only about 26,000 Europeans living in New Zealand at the beginning of the 1850s, it made sense for the country to have six provincial governments. The colonists were living in "settlements...scattered over a distance of about nine hundred miles of latitude,...separated from each other by wide intervals", Grey wrote to the Secretary of State, adding that it was a country occupied in a "scattered and irregular ...manner". Some of the settlements were in closer contact with Australian colonies than with each other. To some extent throughout the 1850s and 1860s the General Assembly of the New Zealand Parliament was simply an arena for provincial rivalries and for clashes of personality among men whose loyalties to their provinces were stronger than their loyalties to New Zealand as a whole.

The provinces actually increased in number during the two decades in which the provincial system was in effect. An act passed in 1858 allowed Hawkes Bay to separate from

Wellington, Marlborough to separate from Nelson and Westland to separate from Canterbury. Southland separated from Otago in 1861 but in 1870 gave up the unequal struggle to remain independent and reunited with its parent province. The provinces survived until 1876 when they were abolished under an act passed in 1875 by a Government which saw provincial rivalries and inequalities of wealth among the provinces as a hindrance to the progress of New Zealand as a whole. The abolition of the provinces left New Zealand with a form of government which was not to be changed significantly until the Upper House was abolished in the early 1950s.

The United States was forged as a nation by the struggle for independence. The New Zealand settlers gained the right to govern themselves without any real struggle. Self-government came with the Constitution of 1852 and responsible government in 1855. In 1853 Dr Featherston, an early Superintendent of Wellington, declared confidently that "the Colonists of New Zealand and their friends at home have fought and won the battle of Constitutional Freedom". A tussle was needed to get the acting Governor to concede the principle of responsible government but it was not much of a fight, a war only of words, not one to create a strong national feeling. The Governor remained a person of considerable power and influence, but after 1856 the ministers — his advisers — were not men of his own choice but men who enjoyed the confidence of the elected representatives of the people. Gradually through the nineteenth century what powers remained with the Governor and the British Government were whittled away. New Zealand was to all intents and purposes independent politically, even while it still gloried in being a colony, part of the British Empire. By 1856, with the cession of responsible government, suggested the author of a History of New Zealand published in 1859, "the child had become a man, proud of his increasing strength, and confident of a splendid future".

Between 1853 and 1876 New Zealand's corridors of power were provincial. The country was governed as a number of separate provinces with their own Provincial Government Buildings. (Inset Pg. 46)
On 6 February 1840 a treaty was signed at Waitangi, in the grounds of the house of the British Resident (Opp. Below and Opp. Top Right) by Governor Hobson, on behalf of Queen Victoria and by a number of Maori chiefs. In return for yielding sovereignty to the Queen, the Maori chiefs were given the rights of British citizens and the undisputed possession of their lands, forests and fisheries. This compact between the two races is regarded as the foundation stone of New Zealand's nationhood.
On 12 February 1840, some Hokianga chiefs assembled at the Mangungu Mission House (Below) where Governor Hobson and his suite were staying, to affix their signatures or marks to the treaty. Over the following months at similar ceremonies in different parts of the country, chiefs of other, but not all the tribes also signed the treaty.
The signing of the treaty cleared the way for a formal proclamation of British sovereignty over New Zealand and for Hobson to be appointed first Lieutenant-Governor, then Governor when New Zealand was separated from New South Wales. (Opp. Top Left)

In 1845 a man who was to play a leading role in the country's life for more than three decades, Sir George Grey, made his first appearance on the New Zealand stage. In the 1860s Grey purchased the Mansion House (Far Left) on Kawau Island north of Auckland, his home for most of the rest of his life. Between 1840 and 1865, Auckland was New Zealand's capital. A substantial house (Below) was built in the mid 1850s as a governor's residence, Hobson's original house having burned down in 1848. As the official home of Governors Gore, Browne and Grey until 1865, it was a centre of the young colony's political and social life.

Between his first and second terms as Governor, Grey served in South Africa. But when his second term as Governor came to an end in 1868, Grey elected to stay in New Zealand, bought property (Bottom) and embarked on a second career as a colonial politician and statesman.

In 1876, a decade after the seat of government was transferred to Wellington, the Government found it necessary to erect the commodious wooden Government Buildings (Top) to house the country's growing number of civil servants.

51

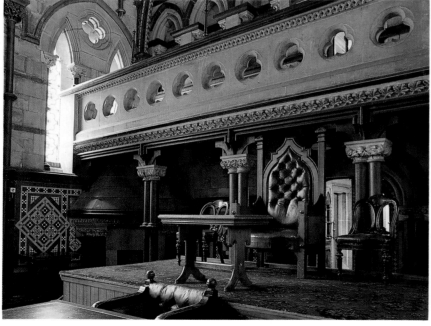

From 1853 to 1876, New Zealand was governed as a number of separate provinces. Canterbury, one of the wealthiest provinces built fine Provincial Government Buildings (Right) for itself. Between 1859 and 1865 the Provincial Council met in a wooden chamber with beautiful Gothic detail. (Top) In 1865 the Council met for the first time in an imposing, ornately decorated stone chamber. (Far Right) The Council sat as a parliament in miniature, presided over by a Speaker whose chair (Above) symbolises the determination of the Provincial Council to be regarded as a real Parliament.

Nineteenth century New Zealanders inherited a deep respect for the rule of law from Victorian Britain. This respect decreed that major towns should have imposing courts of law. Auckland's stately brick Supreme Court (Opp. Bottom Left) was first used in 1868; Dunedin's grand stone Law Courts (Opp. Top Left) were completed in 1902. In small towns throughout the country justice was dispensed in small wooden courthouses like at Ohoke on the Hokianga (Opp. Bottom Right).
A large part of government revenue in the nineteenth century came from custom duties. The small wooden customhouse on the foreshore at Russell (Below) was built in 1870. Aucklands grander stone customhouse (Left) was built, also handy to the waterfront, in 1888.

The Founding Settlements

"The fittest country in the world for colonization ....the most beautiful country, with the finest climate, and the most productive soil; I mean New Zealand."

Edward Gibbon Wakefield 1839

Before 1840 European settlers arrived in New Zealand haphazardly, coming on their own initiative and in small numbers. The few colonists lived mostly in tiny coastal settlements, often where shore whaling stations had been established, or individually as Pakeha-Maori in Maori communities. The year Britain annexed New Zealand was also the year in which organised settlement began, bringing large numbers of settlers to make their homes in different parts of the country. Several of the towns founded in the early 1840s had, by 1850, more European inhabitants than there had been in the whole country when the Treaty of Waitangi was signed.

The figure of one man looms large behind this tide of immigrants: Edward Gibbon Wakefield, the colonial reformer whose vision of transferring whole communities

intact to new lands inspired the founding of a series of colonising companies and associations active first in Australia then in New Zealand. Wakefield's ambition was summed up in a New Zealand Company advertisement, issued in 1839, which stated that the Company's goal was "to transplant English society with its various gradations in due proportions, carrying out our laws, customs, associations, habits, manners, feelings — everything of England, in short, but the soil". (Later Otago was to be founded by men who shared a belief that in a new land "a knot of us can make at any time a Scotland for ourselves".)

One of Wakefield's principles was that land in the colonies should be sold for a 'sufficient' price so that labourers could not, or at least not too quickly, become landowners, depriving the capitalists among the settlers of labour. The money from selling land at a relatively high price would, in addition, be available for spending on churches, schools and public works, so that the settlements did not degenerate into a rough, colonial crudeness. At the same time land had, realistically, to be available at a price which would allow labourers, after a period of saving, to acquire land for themselves. The organisers of the settlement schemes realised that it was only a hope of bettering themselves that would impel many settlers to emigrate to New Zealand.

No New Zealand settlement ever matched Wakefield's ideal. At the time it was suggested that a scheme to transfer a "specimen slice" of English society to New Zealand "was foreign to the democratic genius of Anglo-Saxon colonisation". Wakefield's dream of establishing close-knit agricultural settlements in which people of different classes knew their places and were content to remain in them foundered on the twin rocks of the opportunities in New Zealand to make money in other ways and the determination of the settlers to take advantage of these opportunities. Yet Wakefield's ideas had a profound influence on the way in which New Zealand was settled.

Attempts had been made to plant organised settlements in New Zealand before Wakefield seized on the country as a field for his endeavours. In the 1820s efforts were made to found settlements at Port Pegasus on Stewart Island and on the Hokianga, but neither settlement flourished. Nor were Wakefield-inspired associations and companies the only ones active in the late 1830s. In 1840 the French Nanto-Bordelaise Company sent out a handful of French and German settlers to found Akaroa. But Wakefield's hand was behind most of the major settlements of the 1840s.

The first of the New Zealand Company's settlements was Wellington. Passengers on the company's first immigrant ships landed in January 1840, initially on the exposed beach at Petone. They soon retreated to a more sheltered site on the shores of Lambton Harbour, displacing the Maori who had their

villages there. The company founded a second settlement at Nelson in 1841. In the same year, further north, the New Plymouth Company, an offshoot of the New Zealand Company, founded New Plymouth. Wanganui was founded by company settlers a little later. In 1848, settlers sent out by the Lay Association of Scots founded Dunedin. Two years later, in December 1850, the 'pilgrims' of the Canterbury Association landed at Lyttelton and struggled over the Port Hills to found Christchurch.

Auckland was the only one of the major towns of this first decade of organised settlement which did not owe its origin to a Wakefield inspired or influenced company or association. It was founded in 1841 when the first Governor, William Hobson, decided that the Bay of Islands was not a suitable location for the capital of the infant colony and chose a site on the isthmus between the Waitemata and Manakau Harbours for his seat of Government. In the event Auckland was to remain New Zealand's capital until 1865, although it was dismissed in 1851, by a Wellingtonian, as "a mere section of the town of Sydney transplanted to the shores of New Zealand, filled with tradesmen" which would melt away like a dream if government expenditure ceased.

Gradually through the 1850s and 1860s more settlements were planted, first at other coastal sites, then inland, often as outposts of the original settlements. Small towns grew up in regions like Hawkes Bay, the Wairarapa, Marlborough, South Canterbury and Southland. As they grew some of these towns, like Timaru, attracted immigrant ships directly from Britain. All of New Zealand's major provincial centres had been founded by the end of the 1860s.

In the first three decades of settlement, from 1840 to 1870, tens of thousands of immigrants arrived in New Zealand, most but not all from Britain. New Zealand was a distant and uncertain goal for immigrants in the mid nineteenth century. North America was closer and in many ways a more attractive destination and New Zealand received only a trickle of European migrants compared to the number who merely crossed the Atlantic. Still enough came to New Zealand to ensure it would become a country whose population was overwhelmingly European in origin.

Why did these people uproot themselves, to be borne away so far from home, country and kin, suffering a long, wearisome voyage to the other side of the world, only to have to undertake "the rough work of breaking up a new land"? Most of the motives were common to all who left Europe for different new lands. The Canterbury Association papers of 1850 spoke of "the natural feelings of restlessness and desire for scope and room" which impelled people to emigrate. Samuel Butler thought the emigrants "men...who find the conventionalities of English life distasteful to them, who want to breathe a freer atmosphere" in a land "where the losses and errors of the old life in the old country were to be retrieved".

Many went to New Zealand from a desire to better themselves materially, to pursue "the advantages afforded by a new and uncrowded field for industry or speculation". Even those who lacked the money to buy land of their own immediately on their arrival in the colonies had the prospect of higher wages to draw them. "People do not leave England and go to the Antipodes" observed Butler, ruefully as one seeking workers for his sheep run, "for the same wages which they had at home".

And there was land available. In spite of Wakefield's efforts to prevent labourers becoming too quickly landowners, soon enough in most New Zealand towns working men were living in their own free-hold cottages, perhaps with an acre or two around them. In the countryside could be found significant numbers of small farmers, subsisting at first on just twenty or thirty acres. "There is land enough and to spare in the colonies" George Rennie, one of those who inspired the Otago settlement, told Scots farmers in 1843. In 1847 William Cargill, another associated with the founding of Otago, wrote of New Zealand that "it may safely be affirmed, that the labouring man, with economy and industry, does within three or four years, become himself an owner of property, and independent of working for wages".

That "any man who likes to work and can use his hands will succeed" was the confident, if not always accurate, belief of most settlers.

The agent of the Canterbury Association, John Robert Godley, on the eve of his returning home to England described the two-year-old Canterbury settlement as "a fine field for the exertions of a working man" and spoke confidently of "the rewards which honest industry can reap in a new country". A Taranaki working man bore out these beliefs when he said "the labouring class is as well off here as the nobs are at home. . . A person has a little chance to do something in this part of the world, and that is more than you can do at home".

The colonists drawn by these prospects of a less restricted life and material advancement were neither the very poor nor the very rich. Some poor, though not the poorest, came as assisted immigrants, their passages paid for at least in part by the colonising companies, a practice which provincial Governments, and later the central Government, continued for some decades. Immigrants began to flow to New Zealand during the 'hungry forties' in Britain and some probably did escape near destitution. But most were rather of the upper working and lower middle classes, those described at the time as being members of the 'anxious' or 'uneasy' classes, eager to escape "the din of war. . . the tumult of revolutions. . . the clamour of pauperism. . . the struggle of classes, which wear out body and soul in our crowded and feverish Europe". They were not, most of them driven out by desperation.

Nor was it all a matter of their wanting to benefit themselves materially or enjoy a freer, less troubled life away from Europe's political and social troubles. Colonisation was, to some, simply an adventure. A Canterbury clergyman, Henry William Harper, came to New Zealand in part to enjoy "the romance of personal adventure, and the joy of living a vigorous healthy, simple life;. . . a share in the making of a new colony".

The actual conditions of life in New Zealand were sometimes a rude shock to those who set out for the new land with high, even romantic, expectations. When the Otago settlers arrived in Dunedin in 1848, "the hearts of many. . . failed them while sailing up the harbour on seeing on both sides steep hills densely wooded to their summits". They landed on shore at the site of Dunedin "its surface an entanglement of scrub and flax, without a roof to cover or protect, or a known face to welcome them". They faced a "dread uncertainty as to how or where provisions could be obtained until they could grow their own".

Some became disillusioned because they had left Britain with absurd expectations. Godley remarked that some disappointments in the early days of Christchurch had been "cruel and undeserved" but that many others had been caused "by people's expecting impossibilities". Edward Jerningham Wakefield told the readers of his Advice to Intending Colonists that "among the early Wellington colonists there were some who took their skates with them, and others who imagined they had discovered marble, on seeing a vein of quartz". But even colonists who expected less than the impossible from New Zealand encountered real and disheartening difficulties when they first arrived in Wellington, Nelson, New Plymouth and other early settlements.

The most serious of these intial difficulties was shortage of duly purchased and properly surveyed land for which many had paid before leaving Britain. In some of the settlements the land that was available was often hilly, swampy or of poor quality. A propagandist for the New Zealand Company noted that when the first settlers reached Wellington there was "some surprise at the hilly nature of the country". The reaction of some colonists was rather stronger than that. While they waited for the uncertainty surrounding the New Zealand Company's land purchases to be resolved and for the land to be surveyed, some settlers remained confined to the new towns, depending on Maori farmers for supplies of food, notably pork and potatoes. The gloss must also have been taken off the 'adventure' of colonising a new land by the ache of homesickness. Exploring up the Waimakariri River, Samuel Butler longed "to see some signs of human care in the midst of the loneliness". E.J. Wakefield urged intending colonists to acquire some musical accomplishment before emigrating "as a relief to the solitude of a distant location". In the mid 1860s a Canterbury settler wrote of the distress of living in "a country not only divided from the old by the whole circumference of the earth, but so new that a decade ago it was uninhabited by white men; more than half of it a vacant wilderness; devoid of all historic associations, and even now only occupied by a handful of British, settlers, quite out of touch with the old world".

Disappointments, difficulties and homesickness aside, the settlers were in New Zealand to stay. By the end of the 1850s there were, from one end of New Zealand to the other, several small, rough coastal or near-coastal towns, of a few thousand inhabitants each, behind them hinterlands either empty or still occupied by Maori tribes or the domain of scattered sheepfarmers. Only a few settlers were yet making much money, because the only really profitable investment for capital yet discovered was sheep farming. Most settlers were semi-subsistence farmers, artisans or labourers. Some worked for wages while meeting part of their family's needs for small holdings.

In the towns were men in the professions and in business, importing goods from Britain and Australia. Tradesmen of all description has set up shop — brickmakers, builders, printers, shoemakers. Hotels were doing a flourishing business. Small shopkeepers had opened their establishments.

The less well off among the settlers were living in small cottages with walls of cob, slabs or sawn planks, roofed with thatch or shingles. But already some of the better off were living at a decent standard of comfort in fine large houses. As early as 1841 a Wellington settler had observed that many of the private houses of the most influential settlers were "handsome and wellbuilt". This may have been merely by contrast with the general run of colonial houses, for Christchurch in the early 1850s appeared to one visitor as a "few small woe-begone houses" which "increased rather than diminished the desolate appearance of the landscape". But by the middle of the same decade Auckland, ten years older than Christchurch, presented the appearance of a large town with a mass of houses closely packed together and shops which would not have disgraced a small provincial town in England.

They appeared to some, towns lacking in any sophistication or culture. Yet there was an early striving among New Zealand's settlers to replicate in the new land the amenities, the civilising touches, of the lives they had left behind in Britain. They founded libraries and athenaeums, choral, literary and theatrical societies and newspapers. Military bands were providing popular entertainment. A social round of balls and dinners kept the upper classes of the towns busy. Cricket was soon in vogue and race meetings inaugurated.

But they were still rough, raw colonial settlements. Would-be settlers were advised that what they needed in the colony was "rough, strong, useful" clothing, not finery: "a suit or two of dress clothes lasts a long while in a colony". One sign of the crude conditions of colonial life was the prevalence of drunkenness; it was "fatally common" for men to work hard for a year then blow all their wages in a drinking bout. But if, at the end of the 1850s, New Zealand's towns were still rough, frontier settlements, those who had had a hand in founding them could find cause for satisfaction. One Canterbury colonist, W. Fox, wrote to Godley after Godley had returned to England that he could remember "when...Christchurch consisted of a surveyor's pole stuck upright on the banks of the Avon" and continued: "I know nothing more exciting than to ride on good roads through the midst of colonial villages where less than ten years ago I 'explored' with blankets on my back, without meeting a living thing for fifty to a hundred miles at a stretch". The settlers had begun to make their marks on the land.

The first real homes of most of New Zealand's European settlers were simple gabled cottages, with just one or two rooms, built usually of timber. (Pg 58 Inset)
Before they built their first proper houses, many pioneers lived in smaller, cruder dwellings, like Maxwell Cottage, Waipoua Forest (Left) and the Cuddy on the Te Waimate Station (Top Right) built in 1854 of vertical totara slabs with a thatch roof. Within these primitive first homes was roughly fashioned wooden furniture (Above). Meals were cooked over an open fire, (Top Left) using billies or a camp oven in which bread could be baked. Many of the pioneers lived for months on 'pocket-knife meals of bread and mutton'.

Many settlers quite quickly replaced their first crude huts with weatherboard cottages built of pitsawn timber. Some brought prefabricated cottages with them. The early cottages of the pioneers had a simple charm. One of the French settlers who founded Akaroa in 1840 built himself a small, elegant cottage (Right) in the early 1840s, In 1847 Governor Grey embarked on a plan to erect "mixed hospitals for Europeans and Natives" in Auckland, Wellington, Wanganui and New Plymouth. The Taranaki Colonial Hospital, erected in 1847-48, served mainly Maori patients in its early years, bringing the benefits of European medicine to those Taranaki Maori who came to it (Bottom Left). In the early 1850s members of the Richmond and Atkinson families emigrated together to New Plymouth. In 1855-56, on his bush section on the outskirts of town, Harry Atkinson, (later a premier of New Zealand) sawed the timber for his first New Zealand home, Hurworth. (Below Right) In the town of New Plymouth other members of the families built a stone cottage (Top Left) in 1853, soon after their arrival.

In 1841 John Logan Campbell and his partner William Brown, already residing on the Waitemata Harbour when Governor Hobson chose the site for his new capital city, Auckland, built themselves the simple wooden Acacia Cottage (Below). It was the humble early home of a man who went on to prosper as the city grew and became known as the 'Father of Auckland'.
Most colonial cottages and houses had verandahs, serving as a porch rather than a place to sit.

Many settlers brought furniture and household goods with them. They were able to begin living in comfort and style soon after arriving in their new land. The kitchen (Far Left) might contain a mangle, while in the bedroom (Top) might be a chest or a carpet and in the dairy a butter churn. (Opp. Top) Many settlers, after only a year or two in the country were sitting down to dine (Middle) at a proper dining table on proper chairs. Some settlers, like the Auckland clergyman Vicesimus Lush, brought with them the books and papers they needed to equip libraries and studies (Left) which made the distance between New Zealand and the libraries and colleges of Britain easier to endure.

Many pioneers who came with less or who
made their way more slowly went on living
for many years in rougher conditions, cooking
meals on open fires in a sparsely furnished,
dirt-floored hut built of slabs or cob.
But after a decade or two in New Zealand,
many settlers, including some who had arrived
with very little, were comfortably ensconced in
snug farmhouses, growing some crops and
with their own small flocks of sheep
(Right). Travellers through the isolated Amuri
high country, taken up as pastoral runs from
the 1850s, had to cross high passes between
Nelson and Marlborough and Canterbury on
rough tracks which snow often made
impassable in winter. They found welcome
shelter in the Acheron Accommodation House,
built solidly of cob and with, originally, a
thatched roof in the early 1860s (Above).

Land Wars

"*These lands will not be given by us into ... your hands, lest we resemble the sea-birds which perch upon a rock: when the tide flows the rock is covered by the sea, and the birds take flight, for they have no resting place.*"

Wirimu Kingi 1859

Most European settlers arrived in New Zealand expecting, or hoping, to be able to acquire land of their own. But the Treaty of Waitangi declared clearly that the land belonged to the Maori and that Maori could sell land only to the Government. Before the Government could sell land to the settlers it had to purchase the land from its Maori owners. This was almost always a painstaking, protracted process, because Maori land tenure was a complicated network of individual and tribal rights. Any delay in purchasing land from the Maori while these complexities were unravelled or, far more seriously, any refusal by the Maori to sell their land at all, struck at the main interest of most settlers in coming to New Zealand at all. The complexities of Maori land tenure and the provisions of the treaty seemed largely irrelevant to many of the settlers. Hungry for land, and seeing millions of acres apparently not being used by their native owners, they demanded that the land be opened up for settlement. The belief was widespread that 'civilised men' had the right to step in and take possession of vacant territory which the 'savage tribes' were unable to occupy.

Although much of New Zealand looked empty to the European settlers, there were recognised tribal territories covering the whole country, each tribe having extensive hunting and fishing grounds in addition to the relatively small areas they used for dwelling or growing kumara. Every corner of the country belonged to some Maori or others, and, bound by the Treaty of Waitangi, the Government in the 1840s and 1850s insisted on buying land from all its Maori owners before it was opened up for settlement.

In those decades, in some parts of the country, large areas were sold by their Maori owners. Most of the South Island passed from Maori into European hands; so did large parts of the Wairarapa and Hawkes Bay. But elsewhere efforts to buy land caused trouble, even before the general outbreak of war in the 1860s.

Before 1840, the Maori, not perceiving any threat from the handfuls of traders and whalers on the coasts and probably in most cases not understanding what the transaction meant in European terms, cheerfully 'sold' vast tracts of land for small amounts of European goods. But after settlers began to arrive in numbers, from 1840 on, the Maori came increasingly to realise that they were no longer dealing with a few traders, who were welcome because they were sources of supply of European goods — geese who laid golden eggs. Instead the Maori saw an apparently unending flood of settlers who would, many Maori came to believe, sooner or later take the whole country and perhaps exterminate the Maori as a people. Racist attitudes prevalent among many settlers reinforced Maori fears that their lands and even their racial identity were under threat.

Other causes of misunderstanding and tension contributed to the outbreak of war between the races, local and intermittent in the 1840s, more widespread and prolonged in the 1860s, but at the root of the conflict was that the European settlers wanted land which the Maori increasingly did not want to part with for fear they would ''be swallowed up by the white settlers''.

There was tension over the sale of land from the first days of large-scale settlement when the site of Wellington was being purchased in 1840. ''What will you say...'' a chief Puakawa asked his fellow Maori during these negotiations, ''when many, many white men come here and drive you all away into the mountains? How will you feel when you go to the white man's house or ship to beg for shelter and hospitality, and he tells you

with his eyes turned up to heaven, and the name of his God in his mouth, to be gone, for that your land is paid for?''

On the other side of Cook Strait the first serious clash of arms over land occurred in 1843. The Nelson settlers felt thwarted because Nelson itself lacked sufficient good land for their needs. They therefore greeted with delight the discovery of the rich and extensive Wairau Plains, which seemed to offer a solution to their difficulties. But the Ngati Toa chiefs Te Rauparaha and Te Rangihaeata considered the land theirs and when they attempted to prevent the land from being surveyed a short, sharp affray occurred in which several were killed. A few years later, in 1846, in the Wellington district, Te Rangihaeata took up arms to prevent further loss of land there. Defeated, he retired to an inaccessible pa in the Manawatu. There was skirmishing at Wanganui in 1847 over a disputed land sale.

The best known of the wars of the 1840s was the war in the North, fought in 1845-46 and precipitated by Hone Heke's repeated cutting down of the flag staff at Kororareka. The cause of this war alone was less Maori anxiety about the loss of land than Maori chagrin at the loss of opportunities to trade after the founding of Auckland left Kororareka a backwater. This made the war not typical of most of the wars between Maori and Pakeha.

The late 1840s and early 1850s were times of superficial peace between the races. Newly arrived, Governor Grey brought to an end the conflicts in the North by suppressing Hone Heke and Kawiti, and around Wellington by defeating Te Rangihaeata and taking Te Rauparaha prisoner. Throughout his first Governorship, 1846-53, Grey kept on good terms with the Maori. Land was purchased without provoking serious Maori resistance and Grey actively encouraged the Maori to become farmers in the European mould, providing them with loans and government subsidies for ploughs, mills and vessels to take their products to market. Some Maori prospered selling foodstuffs to the European towns and thriving Maori agricultural communities sprang up in several parts of the North Island.

But Grey's confident assertion to the British Secretary of State for the Colonies that ''both races already form one harmonious community'' was premature. Most Maori still lived in tribal communities, had little contact with settlers, were little affected by Grey's 'civilising' measures and viewed with increasing anxiety the tide of European settlement lapping around their lands. The future of their race seemed at stake, and increasing numbers of Maori began to consider ways of stopping the loss of Maori land to European settlers. ''Men were selling land throughout the island'' a chief told Grey in 1861. ''We thought New Zealand will be gone...we then said, let the land be withheld''. The European rat had already eaten the Maori rat, other Maori noted, ominously.

In 1854 an important meeting was held at Manawapou in South Taranaki at which Maori of several tribes discussed how they could retain the land not yet sold. Old tribal rivalries were submerged as the Maori became increasingly conscious of a 'national' identity and interests, different from those of the European settlers. The 1858 census revealed that Europeans at last outnumbered Maori, fuelling Maori fears. At the end of the 1850s there were 75,000 Europeans and 55,000 Maori in New Zealand as a whole, although in the North Island Maori still outnumbered Europeans by 53,000 to 34,000.

The most telling step taken to give expression to this new sense of Maori identity and new resolve to withhold lands from sale,

and the most alarming to the European settlers, was the setting up of a Maori King. In 1858, a number of important North Island tribes, with the Ngati Haua chief Wiremu Tamehana, 'the Kingmaker', playing a leading role, combined to elect the old Waikato chief Te Wherowhero the first Maori King. "He will be a covering" said Wiremu Tamehana at the time of Te Wherowhero's election "for the lands of New Zealand which still remain in our possession".

But the spark which ignited the land wars of the 1860s was struck not in the Waikato but in Taranaki. Taranaki had hovered on the brink of war for two decades. Soon after the settlement was founded, Governor FitzRoy disallowed most of the New Zealand Company's land purchases in Taranaki, leaving the settlers confined to a few small blocks. As the impatience of the settlers at being confined to these blocks grew, so did Maori unwillingness to sell any more land.

In 1859, prompted by rivalries and antagonisms within the tribe, a minor Te Atiawa chief, Teira, offered land he claimed was his at the Waitara to the Governor, Gore Browne. The chief of the tribe, Wiremu Kingi, and most of its members, refused to allow the Waitara to be sold. Insisting that Teira should be free to sell his land if he wanted to, and with the land-hungry Taranaki settlers clamouring for the sale to be concluded, the Government, early in 1860, proceeded to attempt to survey the disputed block, provoking Wiremu Kingi and his followers first to passive then armed resistance.

The first Taranaki war ended a year later, after a number of pitched battles, when British and colonial troops took the last stronghold of Wiremu Kingi's followers in the Waitara Valley. In 1863, war flared up again in Taranaki, but by then the main focus of conflict had shifted to the fertile and populous Waikato Valley.

In the Waikato in the early 1860s Grey, now Governor for a second time, provoked war by building a military road down from Auckland to the Waikato River from a fear, he claimed, that the Maori were planning to attack Auckland. Taking war to the Waikato was also justified, on the ground that setting up their own king made the Maori rebels, and that any challenge to the Queen's authority had to be put down (although many important chiefs and tribes had never formally acknowledged that authority). Imperial and colonial troops invaded the Waikato, driving the Maori back. A key battle was fought at Rangiriri in 1863. At Orakau in 1864 a small outnumbered band of Maori, led by Rewi Maniapoto, made the heroic stand during which the British were told that the Maori would never make peace — never, never, never. After three days of fighting a remnant of the Maori force made a daring break for safety and the Waikato War was over.

There was fighting also in the Bay of Plenty, but by the mid 1860s the main fighting was over. War continued, a less general but more savage and bitter conflict, into the early 1870s. The later stages of the wars were fought on the European side by colonial troops, for most Imperial troops were withdrawn in 1865-66. On the Maori side the fighting was continued by adherents of the Pai Marire faith (founded by a Taranaki prophet Te Ua in 1862) who became known as the Hauhau. In 1868 the fight was taken up by Te Kooti Rikirangi, founder of the Ringatu religion, who waged bush and guerrilla warfare until 1872, when he was driven into the King Country where he remained in refuge with the still semi-hostile King Movement Maori until he was pardoned in 1883.

A Pakeha missionary, sympathetic to the Maori, described one campaign of these Land Wars with bitter irony, knowing what the war meant to the Maori, as 'One of England's Little Wars'. The wars were, from an imperial point of view, minor incidents in the history of Britain's expansion. They were fought largely on bush and fern; the few fixed engagements occurred when the Maori built pa, taunted the opposing forces into attacking, then

after the engagement escaped, leaving an empty pa to be captured. About 1000 Europeans and Maori who sided with the Europeans were killed; possibly 2000 of the Maori who fought against them died in the fighting.

But although they were 'little wars', they were of great importance in New Zealand's history. Maori resistance to the selling of land was broken. Many Maori retreated into sullen isolation into the areas they still owned, leaving vast tracts of country open to European settlement. In 1863, in the midst of the fighting, the New Zealand Parliament passed an act which provided for the confiscation of land from Maori who had fought against the British and the settlers — a means, the Government claimed, "of deterring other tribes for the future from engaging in rebellion". The confiscation of many thousands of hectares in the Waikato, Bay of Plenty and Taranaki provided land for immediate settlement. Many soldiers who had served in the wars were settled on confiscated land, although those who profited most from the confiscations were Auckland land speculators. But the confiscations left "a smouldering feeling of resentment . . . in the native breast".

The Government also passed, in the early 1860s, Native Land Acts which waived the requirement that land be sold first to the Government, made Maori title to the land they still held individual rather than tribal or communal and set up a Native Land Court to determine who owned Maori land which Europeans wished to buy. A system was inaugurated under which hundreds of thousands of hectares passed from Maori into European hands.

Although defeated in war, and disadvantaged by the new system for land sales, some Maori continued to resist the loss of their land. Their resistance was beaten down by settler Governments, flush with victory and convinced that the progress of European settlement of New Zealand was right and proper, regardless of the wish of some Maori to retain their remaining lands or recover the lands confiscated. At Parihaka, in Taranaki, passive resistance to the building of roads across and European occupation of confiscated lands, inspired by Te Whiti Rongomai, was put down in 1881 by armed policemen and troops facing dancing and singing children.

Continuing resistance to the loss of land was indicative of a surviving Maori spirit, but the forty years after the Land Wars were grim for many Maori. Those who attempted further resistance were stamped on by the authorities. Many others, demoralised by defeat and still subject to the ravages of disease and liquor, allowed the new system of land purchased to strip them of their remaining lands. Their numbers dwindled. Some Maori made the necessary adjustments to live in European society and others still lived in strong, resilient tribal communities. But they were probably a minority. "What is the condition today" asked the New Zealand Times in 1899 "of the Maori who has sold his lands? . . . the remnants on the whole are a poor and miserable lot". It was suggested that all that could be done for the Maori was to smooth the pillow of a dying race.

During the Land Wars of the 1840s, 1860s and 1870s, the muskets of the Maori (Pg 71) were no match for the cannon (Pg 72 Inset) and mortars which the Imperial and colonial troops brought to bear against them. Only three or four thousand lives were lost in all the New Zealand Land Wars, but gravestones tell their stories of individual tragedy (Pg 73). Through the wars, both Maori and Pakeha usually showed respect for the dead and on occasions fighting was suspended to allow each side to bury their dead, and often the dead of their opponents as well.

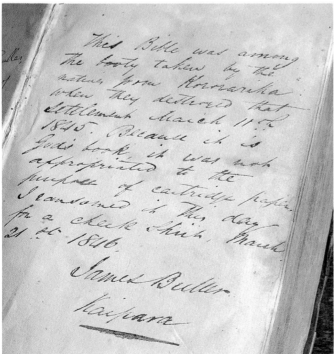

The major war of the 1840s, fought in Northland, was provoked by the Nga Puhi chief, Hone Heke, who repeatedly cut down the flagpole at Kororareka (now Russell) (Above) as a protest against British rule. When Hone Heke captured Kororareka in 1845, much of the town was burned to the ground, but among the buildings spared were Christ Church (Left) and other mission and church buildings.

Maori respect for Christianity, although they were fighting the British who had brought it to New Zealand, was shown by their reluctance to use the paper of bibles and other religious works to make the wads they needed to be able to fire their muskets. (Far Left)

Among those who fought in the War in the North were men from H.M.S. Hazard, some of whom found their last resting places in New Zealand soil. (Below Left)

The first shots in the struggle between Maori and Pakeha over the land were fired in the South Island in 1843. In a brief but bloody incident near Tua Marina (Below Right) several Maori and Pakeha lost their lives. The dispute arose over conflicting land claims.
Maori respect for church buildings persisted throughout the fighting. When Te Kooti descended on the Poverty Bay town of Matawhero in 1868 and sacked it, he spared only the simple kauri building being used as a church. (Below)
The Land Wars were anxious times for the outsettlers whose farms were on the fringes of the settlement, fronting the fern and bush through which the Maori could move swiftly and silently. Guns were kept at the ready. (Right)

SACRED

TO THE MEMORY OF

ARTHUR WAKEFIELD COMMANDER R.N
(A SON OF EDWARD WAKEFIELD ESQR
OF BURNHAM ESSEX) AGENT OF THE
N.Z COMPANY NELSON
HENRY AUGUSTUS THOMPSON
BARRISTER AT LAW POLICE MAGISTRATE
GOVERNMENT REPRESENTATIVE NELSON
GEORGE RYCROFT RICHARDSON
(ELDEST SON OF MAJOR RICHARDSON, OF
BLACKHEATH KENT.)
CROWN PROSECUTOR NELSON
RICHARD ENGLAND CAP 12TH REG.
INFANTRY.
(2 SON OF GEORGE ENGLAND ESQ
OF MITCHAM ABBEY NORFOLK)
JOHN BROOKS INTERPRETER
JOHN COSTER
WILLIAM GARDINER
EDWARD STOKES
JAMES McGREGOR
ELI CROPPER
WILLIAM NORTHAM

WILLIAM BENNETT PATCHETT
(SON OF JONAS TILLOTSON PATCHETT
ESQ. OF HALIFAX YORKSHIRE)
LAND AGENT
JAMES HOWARD, DEAL KENT
GUNNER R.N
N.Z COMPANY'S STOREKEEPER NELSON
SYLVANUS JOHN COTTERELL.
(SON OF HENRY FOWLER COTTERELL ESQ.
OF BATH SOMERSET.)
SURVEYOR.
THOMAS AWDOS MALING.
SON OF WILLIAM MALING OF KIDESIDE
WESTMORELAND)
CHIEF CONSTABLE.
HENRY BOMFORTH.
THOMAS TYRRELL.
ISAAC SMITH
THOMAS PAY.
WILLIAM CLANZEY.
JOHN BURTON.
THOMAS RADCLIFFE

WHO WERE KILLED NEAR THIS SPOT

BY NATIVES OF

NEW ZEALAND.

ON THE 17TH JUNE 1843

F. WAKEFIELD DEL MARCH 1869   W. NORGROVE. BLENHEIM. SCULPR

To defend the exposed European settlements against attack by the Maori, blockhouses were built in strategic places. On the eve of the Waikato War, the most important campaign of the Land Wars, a brick blockhouse was built at Onehunga (Opp. Below) as part of a chain of outposts to protect Auckland.

A wooden blockhouse was built at upper Hutt (Left) in 1860 to help protect Wellington against an attack which never happened.

Even after the fighting petered out in the 1870s, tension between Maori and Pakeha persisted. In the early 1880s, further blockhouses and watchtowers were built at places like Manaia in south Taranaki (Opp. Middle and Opp. Top Right) and Matamata (Opp. Top Left) out of fear that some Maori might again take up arms to prevent the loss of more land

COLD
OFFICE

BANK
OF
NEWSOUTH

Burroughs

The Gold Seekers

"Gold shining like the stars in Orion on a dark frosty night."

Gabriel Read 1861

In the 1860s, while development in the North Island was held back by fighting between Maori and Pakeha, the South forged ahead — winning gold. The first South Island gold rush was to north-west Nelson in 1856, but the small alluvial field was worked intensively for only a few months. Later in the 1850s, explorers and other early travellers on the West Coast and in Otago noted traces of the precious metal in rivers and streams. But it was not until 1861, when Gabriel Read, prospecting in the Tuapeka Stream in Otago, found gold "shining like the stars in Orion on a dark frosty night", that New Zealand's first major gold rush began.

In the two years after Read's discovery and the first rush to the Tuapeka, prospectors pushed further up the Clutha River and its tributaries, discovering rich diggings at

Dunstan on the Clutha itself and up the Shotover and Arrow Rivers. Fortunes were made, overnight, not just by the miners but by "their camp followers so to speak...those who make their livings or fortunes by supplying the wants of the miner". But fortunes were not always made easily. The work was hard with primitive equipment — at first just shovels, goldpans and cradles — and conditions in largely treeless Central Otago were severe. Many miners died in floods or of exposure during the bitter winters. For many, canvas was the only shelter against driving snow.

The first rich takings in Otago were already thinning out when new discoveries lured miners to another, no more hospitable region. In 1864 gold was discovered in Greenstone Creek on the West Coast of the South Island. The rush to this region of dense forests and prodigious rainfall was fully under way by 1865. From Westport to Bruce Bay men were washing the gravels of the rivers and the black sands of the beaches in pursuit of gold. Miners made arduous journeys up the fearsomely gorged and heavily bushed valleys to find rich pockets of gold.

At their backs again were bankers and businessmen who, as in Otago, often did better than the miners themselves. Instant towns sprang up on or near the coast. Hokitika was the largest, but still just a shanty town. In 1866 a new arrival saw from the sea "wooden buildings, tents and corrugated iron structures" in a clearing in the forest on the shore which made up "the metropolis of the new El Dorado — Hokitika". The "metropolis" was a single, low, narrow, irregular street, more than a mile in length, lined with wooden houses, more than eighty of them hotels. The town was built right on the beach, its suburbs a "wilderness of gigantic stumps". In town were "crowds of men, rough and rowdy; their talk of gold; deep and shallow sinking; new rushes; water races and sluicing". "Strings of pack horses, heavily laden" picked their way through town heading for the diggings, where more than 40,000 were at work "getting gold by handfuls". On the diggings the miners made do with even less substantial shelter than in towns like Hokitika; the mining settlements were often mere "calico townships".

A sudden influx of men, some of dubious character, and the temptations offered by the large amounts of gold being taken from the diggings, often on the person of bankers' agents who bought the gold on the spot from the diggers, could have made the goldfields fertile soil for crime. Some crime there was, but the New Zealand goldfields were by and large orderly, if "rough and rowdy". Order was kept by wardens, appointed under government regulations, who settled disputes over claims, framed local laws and saw to it that crime was duly punished. The goldfields worked during the initial Otago and West Coast rushes were alluvial fields. The gold was found in material

washed down over thousands of years, often becoming concentrated in fabulously rich pockets, like the Gabriels Gully of the original find. To win the gold, the miners of the first rushes needed little more than a shovel, goldpan and cradle. This simple equipment worked on the principle that heavier gold is left behind when the lighter gravel, sand and clay in which it is found are washed away. After the rushes, when gold mining settled down to being "a steady, permanent industry", the metal was won in large quantities by applying the same principle in the more sophisticated techniques of sluicing and dredging.

In sluicing, powerful jets of water were used to break up and wash down the gold-bearing material to where the gold could be recovered. Large quantities of water at high pressures were needed and elaborate races and flumes were built to carry the water often long distances to where it was needed. These works needed capital. Gold mining soon became an industry based on companies employing labourers rather than on individual diggers working their own claims. In places, the Government built races and sold water so that individual miners could work their claims by sluicing. Sluicing "gashed and rent" the hills, and an Englishwoman who spent a wet afternoon at the turn of the century among old workings at Ross observed that "where there is gold, all outside beauty must flee away before the digger". The Ross goldfield was unique in New Zealand, for the gold was found in successive "bottoms" in deep alluvial deposits and shafts had to be sunk, and often pumped dry, to reach it. Long after the early diggings were worked out, Ross continued to produce gold. In 1872 a clergyman found the town "by night...as full of work as by day...the whole place lit up with flare lamps".

In dredging, the other large-scale method of recovering alluvial gold, large floating dredges either hauled pay dirt up from the bed of the river or, floating in their own lakes, ate their way across old river flats. Like sluicing, dredging needed capital. It brought another gold boom to Central Otago at the turn of the century, but winning gold was by then a prosaic, organised industry, with fortunes being made from returns on company shares. It was no longer the romantic risky adventure that took the first diggers into wild, scarcely explored parts of the South Island hoping that luck and hard work would win them a fortune.

The North Island, caught up in war, was jealous of the South Island's luck, but before the 1860s were over, the North was sharing in the bonanza. Gold was first discovered in payable quantities in New Zealand on the Coromandel Peninsula in 1852, but the field soon petered out and the main Coromandel and Thames rushes did not take place until the late 1860s. Coromandel was proclaimed a goldfield in 1862, but it was not until the proclamation of the Thames goldfield in 1867 that the goldmining industry of the North Island became firmly established.

Most gold was won on the Thames and Coromandel fields from quartz reefs rather than by washing alluvial deposits. In quartz mining, the gold-bearing rock is crushed in stamper batteries and the gold extracted from the crushed rock by chemical means. From the beginning, this was a matter of organising companies to raise capital for equipment and machinery and to employ workers to dig the tunnels which followed the reefs and to man the batteries. The North Island goldfields lacked the individual romantic excitement of those of the South. Some gold was won in Otago and on the West Coast by mining and crushing quartz, but the South Island quartz fields were not as rich as those of the Coromandel. The Waihi mine, opened in 1878, went on producing gold well into the twentieth century. The gold rushes were more than just an exciting interlude in New Zealand's history. They had a profound impact on the country, not least for bringing to New Zealand different sorts of persons from those who came to the 'organised' settlements. The discovery of gold drew to New Zealand "lusty, powerful fellows, given to occasional sprees, with something sailor-like in their comradeship, rowdy but honest, and free from crime". The diggers were "a hardy class of people...remarkable for their sturdy independent air and manner...for the most part...restless, stirring, energetic fellows". It took a measure of restlessness and energy to come to New Zealand at all, but in the goldminers these characteristics were particularly marked.

At the time, not all of those drawn by the lure of gold were entirely welcome. An infusion of the "convict element" was suspected and it is likely that some liberated convicts did find their way to Otago in the great rush from Australia in 1862. Large numbers of the goldminers who came in the 1860s had moved on from California, to Australia and then to New Zealand. The gold rushes also drew in their wake an entirely different ethnic group, the Chinese, some of whom, by hard work and frugal living, made small fortunes working systematically over ground already fossicked through by European miners. A writer familiar with the Otago goldfields observed that "taken as a whole the heathen Chinese are a very hard-working, industrious, steady people, generally of a lighthearted, merry disposition", but also noted that a "spirit of antagonism to the celestials" showed itself on the goldfields. The Chinese miners generally lived in their own communities on the edge of the goldmining towns, keeping to themselves. Many yearned eventually to return to China, but many also stayed.

The impact of the gold rushes can also be seen in the growth of New Zealand's population. Because of the Otago rushes, Dunedin became, overnight, New Zealand's largest city. Between 1861 and 1863 Otago's population exploded from 12,600 to more than 60,000. In 1863, at the height of the Otago rushes, more people arrived in New Zealand than there had been Europeans living in the whole of the country just ten years earlier. On the West Coast, Hokitika was briefly, in the late 1860s, New Zealand's leading export port. By 1867 there were between 30,000 and 35,000 people on the Coast where in 1860 there had been probably fewer than 100. "Nothing" observed a West Coast clergyman "populates a howling wilderness like gold".

Over-all, the European population of New Zealand trebled in the 1860s. Between 1861 and 1867 (years in which censuses were taken) the total European population rose from under 100,000 to more than 218,000. In the same period the population of the North Island rose from just over 41,000 to a little below 80,000 while that of the South Island leapt from just over 52,000 to more than 138,000.

Gold also earned New Zealand much of the money which paid for its progress in the 1860s. For every year from 1861 to 1870 gold was the single most important export from New Zealand, earning the country more than all its other exports put together. The spur to development from gold was felt in many areas of New Zealand life. The opening of the West Coast goldfields prompted the Canterbury Provincial Government (Westland was then part of Canterbury) to have a road built through the Southern Alps, across Arthur's Pass, in 1865. A thousand men toiled through a bitter winter to cut a coach road in less than a year. In the event, most of the gold won on the West Coast went by ship to Dunedin or Melbourne, but for the next seventy years this was the only route for wheeled traffic from one coast of the South Island to the other. It was one of the country's many legacies from gold.

Some early diggers made their fortunes with no more than a shovel and a gold pan. (Pg 82 Inset) But not all the gold was won so easily. Tunnels had to be dug to reach deep alluvial deposits or reefs of gold-bearing quartz. (Bottom) Heavy machinery was needed to provide water at high pressure for sluicing (Left) or to crush quartz rock (Below & Far Left) so that the gold could be recovered.

Goldmining was hard work and the miners earned the relaxation they found in the hundreds of hotels that sprang up on the goldfields. The earliest hotels were rough shacks of calico and tin, but on the longer-lasting fields substantial hotels were built to cater to the miners' thirst for alcohol and entertainment and their need for accommodation. St Bathans acquired its mudbrick Vulcan Hotel (Previous Page) in 1869. Hotels at Styx (Right), Cardrona (Above) and Dunstan (now Clyde) (Far Right) all did a roaring trade in goldmining days.

Large amounts of gold, many disappointed diggers, drink and plain ruffians might have seemed a recipe for lawlessness, but the New Zealand goldfields were mostly quite orderly. Jails were, all the same, needed in the gold towns. Prisoners travelling under escort from the Dunstan diggings to Dunedin spent a cold, uncomfortable night in the Styx jail (Far Left & Pg 94). Arrowtown's solid jail (Bottom Centre & Middle) threatened lawbreakers with heavy iron doors shutting off badly ventilated cells.

On the fringes of many goldmining towns
were the usually humble huts (Top and Right)
of frugal and hardworking Chinese miners.
At the time of the first rushes, the diggers
threw up crude, makeshift shelters (Above Left)
or made do with tents to leave as much time
as possible to pan for gold.

The goldfields were administered by Goverment-appointed wardens, to whose offices (Far Right) miners came to register their claims or have their disputes settled.

Most gold won by the miners found its way into the hands of bankers (Below) who often did just as well as those whose hard work won the gold. Banks were often the most prominent buildings on the streets of gold towns (Bottom Right). But hotels, stables (Bottom Left) shops, and the offices of goldmining companies (Right) formed to raise capital for the machinery needed to recover hard-to-get gold were also strung out along the single main streets.

After the frenzy of the first rushes, the miners who stayed behind settled down and built themselves more permanent houses, of stone in Bendigo (Left) and Fruitlands (Below & Top) and of wood in Arrowtown. (Above)

99

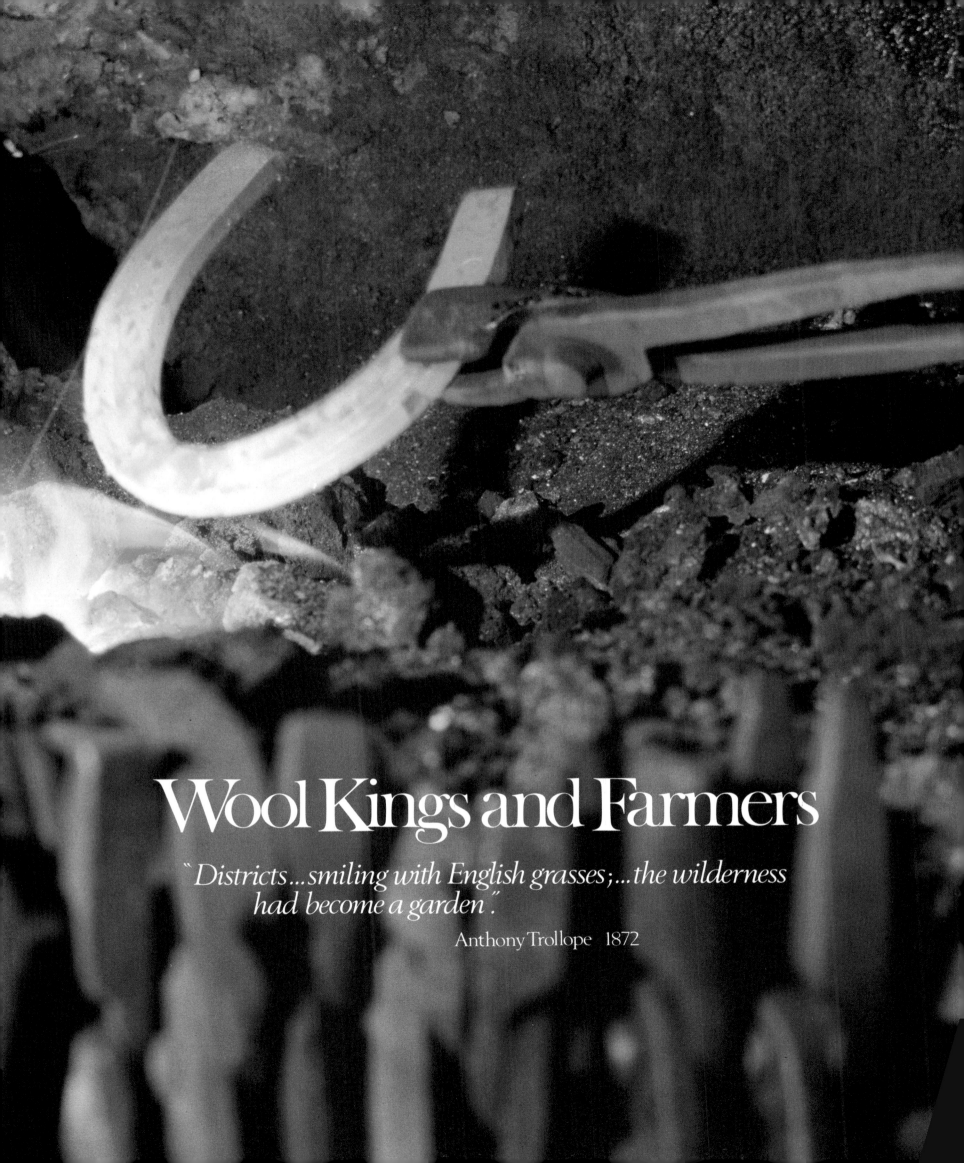

Wool Kings and Farmers

"Districts...smiling with English grasses;...the wilderness had become a garden".

Anthony Trollope 1872

From the earliest days of organised European settlement, most Pakeha New Zealanders made their living not from gold but from the land. A surgeon who accompanied Captain Cook observed that ''the only obstacle to this being one of the finest countries upon earth is its great hilliness, which, allowing the woods to be cleared away, would leave it less proper for pasturage than flat land, and still more improper for cultivation''. Hills and forests in many parts of the country did indeed present formidable obstacles to the New Zealand settler endeavouring to establish a farm. The story of the small holder struggling to transform steep, bush-clad hills into pasture is perhaps the main story of nineteenth century New Zealand.

town as well, employed servants, visited England and sent their sons there for their education. Some found the lack of deference of other colonists towards them galling, but this did not prevent them, as a class, from dominating the political life of several provinces and often of the country as a whole for several decades.

As they prospered, many pastoral runholders bought up the freehold of vast areas of land they had initially leased. They were helped to do so, paradoxically, when Governor Grey, trying to make it easier for ordinary people to become small landowners, lowered the price of land. Where they could purchase outright all the land they had leased, the runholders resorted to 'spotting', 'grid-ironing' and 'dummying' to maintain their grip over large areas.

But the first to make farming pay well in New Zealand avoided these obstacles by taking advantage of the natural grasslands of the Wairarapa, Hawkes Bay and, especially, the South Island. Onto these grasslands they turned flocks of sheep. (Some of these areas have, to this day, proved to be no use for anything else but running sheep.) The rough tussock and scrub were burnt by the early runholders to encourage the fresh growth on which the flocks thrived. ''Burnt feed means contented and well-conditioned sheep'' wrote Samuel Butler, who doubled his capital in four years as a Canterbury runholder.

Sheep were first turned out to pasture in the Wairarapa in 1844. From there pastoralism spread across Cook Strait into Marlborough, then down into Canterbury and Otago until, by about 1860, the Canterbury foothills, the Mackenzie Basin and inland Otago had all been taken up in often vast sheep runs, held on favourable terms of lease from governments anxious to foster an industry that promised to generate wealth for the new settlements.

The Canterbury settlement was scarcely six months old when Godley reported the opinion that ''there is no field of investment now open in the world at once so safe and so profitable as pastoral husbandry in New Zealand''. Sheep farming became ''the real and in truth the only source of (the colony's) prosperity''. The Wakefield principles on which Canterbury had been founded were meant to discourage extensive pastoral settlement but were wisely modified by Godley to allow settlers to lease large areas of land at relatively low rentals as sheep runs. Many who did so were Australians. The flocks to stock Canterbury — the pre-eminent pastoral province — came largely from established flocks in Nelson and Marlborough. In Canterbury, sheep farming became not just an occupation but an obsession of some colonists. ''A mountain here is only beautiful if it has good grass on it . . . If it is good for sheep it is beautiful, magnificent and all the rest of it; if not, it is not worth looking at'' wrote Samuel Butler.

Great fortunes were made from wool, grand houses built and almost aristocratic ways of life adopted by the great runholders. But in the early days the runholders led rough, isolated lives, ''beyond the pale of civilisation'', sheltering under canvas or in rough cob cottages, existing on a monotonous diet of mutton and bread or 'damper'. Their lives appeared to Butler ''a kind of mixture of that of a dog and that of an emperor''. Sheep farming was, as well, a risky business and not all who leased land on which they turned out flocks survived to become wealthy station owners. The dreaded disease scab, fluctuating prices for wool, snowstorms or floods spelt ruin for many.

But those who did prosper became very wealthy indeed — a ''Southern Gentry'' one historian has called them. They built grand homesteads on their stations and often elegant houses in

As their holdings grew, Scottish shepherds who 'kept the boundaries' gave way to ''miles upon miles of wire fences''. In the 1870s and early 1880s, many Canterbury and Otago station owners made huge profits in a wheat bonanza, employing hundreds of men as contractors or as seasonal labourers to cultivate and harvest vast paddocks of grain.

Although they loom large in the early years of some South Island provinces, the lessees and then owners of large sheep runs were a small minority of the settlers, even in Canterbury. Most Canterbury settlers lived in Christchurch or in an agricultural, as opposed to pastoral, fringe around the town. This fringe was one of small holdings ''chiefly in the hands of labouring men who have made a little money, bought land, and cultivated it themselves''. In Otago, most of the farmers among the first settlers had small holdings on the Otago Peninsula or on the plains between Dunedin and Balclutha.

It was a struggle in the early years to make farming on these small holdings pay. Butter, cheese, vegetables and other agricultural products were sold in the towns or occasionally in Australia, but the markets were small and uncertain. With the gold rushes the demand within New Zealand for farm products grew, but many small farmers still had to supplement their income from farming by working for wages.

There were other difficulties to overcome, besides lack of markets. In Canterbury, when settlers pushed out beyond the immediate fringe of Christchurch into the Ellesmere district, they encountered ''a maze of marsh and bog'' which exacted the hard labour of digging drains before it became productive farmland. But by 1868, when Lord Lyttelton visited the Ellesmere district, he saw across the plains a ''few homesteads at wide intervals like oases in the desert, marked by small buildings and trees growing up around them; . . . mud cottages here and there where shepherds live; a few corn ricks scattered about; some invisible wire fences dividing properties''. It was a landscape of small farms. In two decades, even in a province dominated by great sheep runs, small farmers, growing crops, keeping a few cows or running a few sheep, had already established a foothold from which they were not to be shaken.

The carving of farms from North Island bush country demanded even more laborious effort of the settlers. The effort began in the 1850s when parties of settlers walked over the Rimutaka hill from the Hutt Valley and took up bush sections in the Wairarapa. It was to continue until well into the twentieth century. Bush settlers faced on their land ''a tangled mass of luxuriant vegetation'' presenting ''rather a formidable appearance to the English axeman''. Fire and axe gradually ate into this primeval forest until travellers could see ''on the outskirts of the bush . . . the clearing of some industrious settler,

the rough log fence...the white bleached stumps sticking up here and there through the green luxuriant grass...the rude hut built of the black stems of the tree fern''.

Where North Island land for settlement was not covered in bush, it, too, was often swampy. The huge Piako swamp was drained at great expense by the Waikato Land Association and by the mid 1880s was ''a rich plain dotted with cattle, homesteads and plantations of trees''. Drainage was often the work of companies or moneyed land developers who then sold farms to individual settlers. Clearing a bush section was usually an individual occupation. It was back breaking toil, but the rewards gradually came. After a year or two under canvas or in a punga hut, most settlers would build for themselves and their families a one or two room slab cottage with a shingle roof. After a few more years, the settler's family would be living in a more substantial weatherboard cottage or house, usually with a verandah and a corrugated iron roof. Near the house would be farm buildings, a woolshed, a dairy (perhaps built of brick), a hen run. But the comforts of a proper farmstead came only after toil and privation, shared by men and women alike. Many pioneer women led lonely lives in slab whares surrounded by bush and mud. Many had to walk long distances along bush tracks to obtain supplies.

Conflict between the interests of these small farmers and those of the station owners provided an edge to New Zealand politics in the nineteenth century, when many clashes in Parliament were based on merely personal or local rivalries. A consistent and ardent champion of the small farmer was Sir George Grey. The future prosperity and welfare of New Zealand, he wrote as early as 1848, would depend on ''persons who have acquired or are acquiring small properties on which they intend to reside themselves during the remainder of their lives and to settle them on their children''.

As Governor, Grey in 1853 lowered the price of land in an effort to encourage the landless to take up small holdings, though the actual consequences of this step were not what Grey intended and much land passed into the hands of speculators and large landowners rather than small farmers. Twenty years later, in the 1870s, Grey, as a politician, continued his efforts to ''save the country from that gigantic evil of an aristocracy with enormous tracts of land'' and to frame ''laws under which every family may hope to obtain its home and its land''.

''Much wordy warfare'' was waged in Provincial Councils and the General Assembly over the land laws, the cry 'land for the people' being matched on the side of the squatocracy by the cry 'preserve vested rights'. Some Provincial Councils, until they were abolished in 1876, made token efforts at least to frame laws regulating land purchase and land holding which would help the small man onto the land. In Otago a deferred payment system was introduced to help former gold diggers purchase their own farms.

Promoting settlement of the country by small farmers was one of the goals of the leading politician, Julius Vogel, who in 1870 launched a grandiose scheme to develop the country. Immigration was to supply the people to break in new land and public works, especially railways, to make it easier for them to get their farm products to markets. Some Vogel immigrants arrived as community groups who together carved farms and townships out of the bush. In the 1870s northern Wairarapa and southern Hawkes Bay were broken in by parties of Scandinavians who lived first in slab huts on 40-acre sections of dense bush, surviving on roadmaking contracts while they worked on ''getting the bush down''. By the mid 1880s parts of these districts were ''splendid tract(s) of land, dotted over the thriving townships, rich in highly cultivated farms, and teeming with sheep, cattle and horses''. Further in the backblocks the bush was still standing, with ''occasional stump clearings, rising settlements and sequestered homesteads''. In other areas small

farm associations promoted the opening up of further blocks to settlement. In Northland, groups of Dalmations dug for kauri gum, leading ''isolated and fearfully hard'' lives out on the gumfields, which they slowly transformed into farmland. The gum provided ready cash while the farms were being established.

Small farmers suffered as much, if not more than, wealthy station owners in the slump of the late 1870s and 1880s which followed the Vogel boom. But in the middle of the slump occurred an event which was to affect profoundly, for the better, the prospects of New Zealand's small farmers. In 1882 the first cargo of frozen meat and butter was shipped from New Zealand to England. For the next hundred years the refrigerated trade to England was to provide a sure market for the products of New Zealand's small farmers — meat as well as wool from sheep, butter and cheese from cows.

Dairying was, pre-eminently, a pursuit of small farmers, especially on cleared bush country in Taranaki, the Waikato and other North Island districts. With the rise of dairying, butter and cheese factories began to appear in the countryside, many of them owned by farmers' co-operatives. More scattered were the creameries to which farmers brought their milk for separation, waiting for the skim milk which they took home to feed calves and pigs.

At the end of the nineteenth century bush country was still being opened up for settlement. Pioneers in the North Island backblocks were still burning and clearing forest and scrub, sowing pasture in the ash-rich soil and fencing their land, just as their predecessors in more accessible parts of the country had been fifty years before. In 1841 Charles Heaphy found the typical Port Nicholson settlers ''always employed either in the cultivation of the ground, or on fresh clearings; and, while improving his property, ...subsisting on the produce of that portion of it already in cultivation''. Many New Zealanders, fifty years later, were still doing exactly the same. Thanks to the markets opened up by refrigeration, however, the latter-day pioneers were generally able to enjoy sooner than the first settlers ''the advantages of a grateful soil''.

To serve the country's growing numbers of small farmers, rural townships grew up. Each had their shops, schools, churches, banks, library, hotels and blacksmiths' shops. Some also had a dairy factory or saleyards, or their own post office. They were hardly the picturesque villages of Europe. One English visitor, describing the central Hawkes Bay township of Otane, complained to her family that the town was ''built entirely of wood and all the roofs nearly are made of corrugated iron. Still as the houses have nearly all verandahs and pretty creeping plants up them it doesn't look as ugly as one might imagine''. Some of the townships were, while the land around them was still being cleared, ''romantically located'' in ''a...clearing in the midst of what was recently a virgin forest''.

Poor transport and communications obliged the farming folk and those in country townships to make their own entertainment. There were local race meetings, annual sports in the domain and, in areas where sawmilling was a local industry; axemen's carnivals. The settlers overcame the isolation of being a scattered population by gathering in the townships, in the hotel on a Saturday, in church on Sunday morning. Lord Lyttelton, visiting Southbridge in 1868, ''attended a very nice little church which had been built even in these solitudes. It is a great comfort to the scattered farmers about; and it was curious to see them collecting together round the church in small gigs and drays, slowly moving across the plain from all points of the compass. The church, wooden as usual, but very seemly...'' A Canterbury clergyman wrote to an English friend of a church he thought would seem to the friend ''an ecclesiastical barn with its rough, open roof, unlined wooden walls, and no chancel. But'' he added ''it is spacious and well cared for, and well attended''.

The townships were self-sufficient because they had to be — New Zealand's roads for most of the nineteenth century remained appalling. Heavy loads were carried on waggons, often drawn by bullocks — a bullock was "a good, slow, steady, patient slave if you let him take his own time about it". Everybody rode — the minister from township to township for services, the children to school. To the settler a horse was "carriage...coach...and...railway train". Horse-drawn traps, gigs, coaches and other vehicles carried people in greater comfort or in greater numbers. In many parts of the country, rivers were the travellers' greatest hazard. Governor Grey, after nearly being tipped out of a canoe into the Kaniere River, remarked that he had "had many a narrow shave in African rivers, but never quite so close a thing as that". It was a red-letter day for a township when the river separating it from the nearest town or city was bridged, often years after a district was first settled.

In parts of the country, railways were more important than roads. In the 1870s, during the flurry of public works of the Vogel era, a number of rural branch lines brought the benefits of travel by train to many country districts. But on one Canterbury branch line it took the train "two and a half hours of solid crawling" to do thirty miles. Even those rural towns and townships linked to a larger centre by rail remained self-contained and self-sufficient communities, flourishing in the late nineteenth and early twentieth centuries in a way they have not since.

Stone barns (Pg 102 Inset) and wooden woolsheds (Pg 103) were built by the New Zealand pioneers so they could work their newly broken in land.
By the 1870s some farmers, like the widely travelled artist and politician Sir William Fox, had prospered sufficiently from farming to be able to build large, sturdy farmhouses for themselves (Following Pages). Fox named his house Westoe, like many other settlers nostalgically using the name of the English parish from which he had come.

In the South Island, fortunes based on wool enabled large runholders to build huge mansions, like the Campbell homestead at Otekaieke (Opp. Top Right). The stables at Otekaieke (Opp. Top Left) were far larger than the houses of the small farmers. But many runholders, like those on the Galloway Station in Central Otago, lived much more modestly (Below) than the Campbells of Otekaieke.

Parts of the North Island, like most of the South Island, also had great runs and stations whose owners made fortunes, mostly from wool. The owner of Oruawharo in Hawkes Bay graduated from the primitive bark hut he occupied in 1861 to an imposing wooden house (Right) built in the 1870s. In its drawing room was an elaborately detailed wooden ceiling (Below). Though often far out in the country, the opulently furnished drawing rooms (Pg 109) and even the well-furnished nurseries (Bottom) of these great homesteads provided comfort and luxury of which most New Zealanders, in town or country, could only dream.

*Wealth from business enterprises in town was often
ploughed back into buying landed estates and
building grand country houses. A Nelson
businessman, William Nicholson, built Woodstock
(Above) on his country acres in the 1850s.
In Southland, the fine stone house Wantwood (Opp.
Top Left) was built in 1886-87 after an earlier
homestead, on a large run taken up in the 1850s, had
burned down.
In the homesteads of these large estates or runs the
bedrooms (Right and two Opp.) matched
the main living rooms for comfort and luxury in
many cases.*

Broadgreen (Opp. Top) was built of cob in the mid 1850s by a Nelson businessman who had made his first money from land in Canterbury. It was typical of the homes of the lucky few colonial gentlemen of property who dined in splendour (Above and Top) and had comfortable studies (Opp.) to which they could retreat.

115

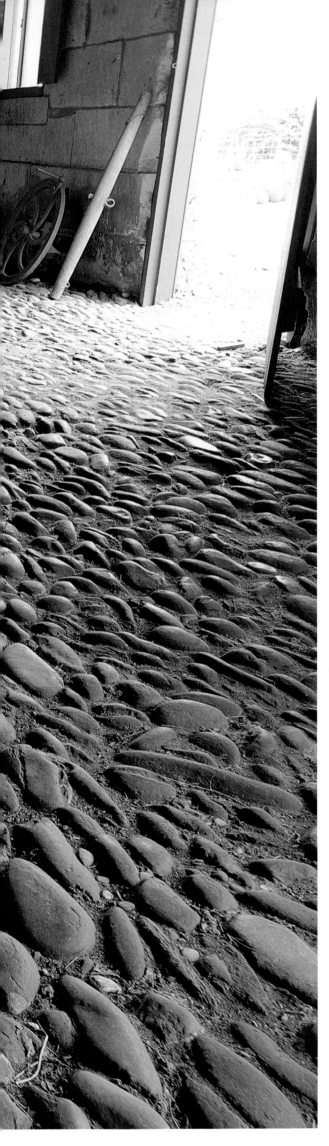

Usually some distance from the house on the large estates were the farm buildings from which the estates were worked, most importantly the stables for the horses which drew ploughs, farm machinery and wheeled vehicles and were ridden for work and pleasure. On the Galloway Station in Central Otago the simple stables (Left) were built of stone; at Brancepeth in Hawkes Bay the stables (Below), built of wood, included a coach house. (Far Left) Stable floor Totara estate.

In the early days of the great runs, the flocks were tended by shepherds until, gradually, the runs were fenced. Wood was so scarce in Central Otago that at Cottesbrook even the fence posts were stone (Above). All the large sheep stations had rough quarters (Right) where the itinerant gangs of shearers lived while the vast flocks were shorn.
After shearing, the wool had to be carted often long distances to port on huge horse or bullock drawn wagons (Top Right). Only in later years were the many rivers between most sheep runs and their ports bridged (Middle Right).

119

On the largest sheep runs during the frantic shearing season, when all was 'stir and bustle' on the stations, 20 or 30 shearers would clip up to 3000 sheep a day. The great woolsheds built of wood (Far Left) or stone (Above) were in effect factories for shearing the huge flocks. (Left) Door catches on a shed, Oturehua.

At the opposite end of the scale from the great sheep stations were the small bush sections of the North Island settlers. Before the land could be farmed, dense bush had to be cut down by axe or saw (Left). But once enough timber had been pitsawn for house and outbuildings, fire was often used to ease the toil of clearing the bush.
In the far North, while settlers worked at breaking in their farms they supplemented their meagre incomes from farming by digging for kauri gum which they sold to a local gum dealer (Above & Right). The dug over swamp lands of former gumfields often became good farmland.

Living in mansion and farm cottage alike, many nineteenth century New Zealanders drew their water from hand pumps in the yard (Above) and cooked on wood or coal burning stoves (Left). (Above Left) House built in Motueka around 1870 by a Norwegian seaman who jumped ship in Nelson. (Far Left) Mansion house kitchen, Kawau Is.

Pioneering life was often hard, but the land was soon providing even the poorest with ample food (Previous Page). One station owner complained of his workers that men "who at home lived on porridge. . .from one end of the year to the other expect to receive tea and meat three times a day".

Most nineteenth century rural New Zealanders lives in houses or cottages far smaller than the mansions of the great runholders. The interiors of these cottages (Right and Top) were simple and functional, but not lacking completely in comfort and style. (Above) Gatekeepers cottage Corwar Lodge, Barrhill.

Most of the settlers on the land built their simple, gabled houses of wood, but where wood was scarce stone or cob (earth) served instead. Although all simple, these homes of the ordinary pioneers were built also in a great variety of styles, with whatever decoration the slowly prospering settler could afford.

Like those of the great estate owners, the farmsteads of the small settlers also had their complement of farm buildings, smaller than woolsheds and stables of the great estates, but sturdy and functional buildings. (Opp. Top) Greytown stables, (Left) Hop Kiln, Dovedale, (Below) Sledge hut. In the farm buildings on the Totara Estate, near Oamaru (Opp. Bottom), the New Zealand freezing industry was born. The industry, opening overseas markets for meat, butter and cheese as well as wool, greatly improved the prospect of the country's small farmers.

Death haunted the lives of the pioneers and around their simple wooden churches or in the cemeteries on the outskirts of their townships were soon many gravestones telling of death by drowning in the country's tempestuous rivers or by accident in the bush as the rough, dangerous work of clearing forests of enormous trees went ahead. Many settlers were beyond the reach of doctors and early gravestones frequently tell poignant stories of whole families of youngsters carried off by disease or of women dying in childbirth. So the soil of New Zealand claimed many immigrants, often before their hopes of a better life in a new land had been fulfilled.

The parish church in countryside and township
was a source of spiritual consolation for the
settlers, and also an important gathering place
for people who led often lonely lives on
isolated farms.
Churches were the first substantial public
buildings erected in many districts. Holy Trinity,
Lyttelton (Far Right) was built only ten years
after the Canterbury settlement had been
founded and treasures a communion plate
(Right) which the Canterbury Pilgrims brought
out with them on the First Four Ships in 1850.
(Top) Minniedale Chapel, Port Albert, Kaipara.
(Above) St Johns Arrowtown.

Settlers travelling the long, slow distances between towns in the nineteenth century spent their nights on the road in accommodation houses or hotels (Above Right).

At these accommodation houses or hotels there was stabling for the travellers' horses (Top Right) if they were lucky enough to be riding and not on foot. A cast horse-shoe could be replaced at the forge (Above) if necessary.

Country towns, their main streets (Left) lined with public buildings and the premises of shopkeepers and tradesmen (Below) met the needs of the settlers for special services or goods. Many of these country towns were far larger and busier places in the nineteenth century than they are today.

As the nineteenth century advanced to its end, New Zealand's settlers built many different sorts of buildings. Their doors reflect the variety of purposes the buildings served. Some, by the century's end, were distinctively New Zealand doors, made in New Zealand and already unlike the doors of the home countries from which the settlers had come (Following Page).

In country stores in a hundred townships, farming settlers bought the manufactured goods and things like tea, sugar and salt which they could not produce on their farms. Many settlers, though, were very nearly self-sufficient.

The settlers came to town not just to shop (Opp. Top) but to do their banking (Below), to post their letters (Right), perhaps to members of their families still living in Europe or, at the public library (Opp. Middle) to catch up on the latest news or perhaps borrow the latest novel newly arrived from England. The school to which the settlers sent their children (Opp. Bottom) might be in the local township, or right out in the country for the children of out settlers.

Life in the Towns

"Outwardly the place is as civilised as if it were a hundred years old;
well-paved streets, gas lamps, and even drinking fountains
and pillar post-offices."

Lady Barker 1865

Vogel's programme of immigration and public works, inaugurated in 1870, saw the frontier of settlement pushed further into the North Island's hill and bush country. It also ushered in an era of growth and development for New Zealand's towns. In the 1870s New Zealand's population doubled to reach half a million. 115,000 newcomers came as assisted immigrants. A good number of these went out onto the land, but a good number, too, settled in towns and cities. "Townships which only a few years before comprised but few dwellings — and those of an insignificant kind — soon developed into towns of importance; and towns of only a few thousands of inhabitants were as speedily transformed into cities, possessing edifices which would do credit to older established countries."

By 1881 more than 190,000 of the total European population of 490,000 lived in 65 boroughs. Dunedin had 40,000 inhabitants, Christchurch 25,000 and Auckland and Wellington both more than 20,000. By that time, stimulated first by the gold rushes, then by the rapid development of the 1870s, these four main centres had become cities of some size and pretension. One who recalled that in 1857 Dunedin had been a place where there were "neither theatre nor amusements of any kind, and nothing to any extent worth naming of what is usually called society" found Dunedin 1879 "a very intellectually active little place, a very city of pleasures in its way, and devoted to follies and lightness quite more than enough." A visitor found Dunedin's heart "throbbing with the deep pulsations of active commercial life." By 1880 a number of New Zealand cities had reached what yet another observer called "the hansom-cab pitch of civilisation".

The growth of the cities was perhaps most evident in their architecture. By the late 1880s Auckland had "completed its transition from the wooden age" and was "well-advanced in the age of brick". Though Christchurch was "not nearly so advanced in the age of brick and stone as Auckland" it had "some stately edifices that would grace any metropolis". The newcomer from "the home country" was "often astonished to find nearly everyone, both rich and poor, living in wooden houses". Many of even the finest houses, the town residences of large landowners and the homes of the urban elite of business and professional men, were built of wood. So were some larger public and commercial buildings, particularly in Wellington, where fear of earthquakes made people hesitate to build in masonry. But elsewhere substantial buildings of stone and brick were giving New Zealand's cities a permanent, established appearance. They were public buildings of different sorts, commercial premises, churches and schools. The passing of the Education Act in 1877, which provided for compulsory, free and secular education, further stimulated the building of large public schools which some Provincial Governments had already begun. Even the anonymous colonist who had so jaundiced a view of New Zealand as to write a book called *Taken In* observed that "Government schools are numerous and are fine buildings considering the extreme youth of the country".

The inhabitants of the cities could, if they chose, lead active intellectual and cultural lives. By the 1880s both Dunedin and Christchurch had universities housed in handsome stone edifices built specially for the purpose. Nearby each were substantial museums. In that decade Auckland erected an imposing building for its Free Library and Public Art Gallery. But probably more city dwellers enjoyed the races than

patronised the library and art gallery. By the late 1880s, Auckland's racecourse at Ellerslie had two grandstands, the main one seating 5,000 persons. It was to be expected that horse racing would be a favourite amusement in a country where riding was a necessary accomplishment for most, at least beyond the cities, and that race meetings would be important events on the social calendar. One traveller found in the mid 1870s that nearly every township had "a piece of adjacent land reserved ... for a race-course".

These increasingly grand cities were gaining many amenities, but they were still, by modern standards, primitive places. In the 1870s, Dunedin's roads in winter were "perfect quagmires of most tenacious yellow clay, rendering travelling on foot almost impracticable". Ladies wanting to attend social gatherings had, on occasion, to travel, decked out in their finery, by bullock sledge. Christchurch's situation, on flat, formerly marshy ground, made drainage a problem and epidemics of diseases, the result of poor drainage, were a constant worry. The Christchurch Drainage Board was established in 1875 when a serious epidemic of typhoid threatened. Some sewers were laid in the early 1880s and over the city as a whole the death rate from disease fell dramatically, but the work was discontinued because it was costing too much and even into the 1890s typhoid, diphtheria and other diseases continued to take a heavy toll in Christchurch. Drains emptying into natural watercourses and pollution of the wells from which many citizens drew their water remained an especially serious problem in the crowded working class suburbs of Sydenham and Linwood. But as the nineteenth century drew to a close improvements were made in providing basic services to the main centres.

The four main centres were not the only towns to grow through the 1870s and 1880s. In mid-Canterbury Ashburton, by the mid-1880s, was a flourishing town where a little more than twenty years before "was only a bullock teamster's camp, boasting merely a rude publichouse, a blacksmith's shop and a police hut. Now it is a gas-lit town with spacious streets, lined by shops, public buildings, hotels, churches, schools, a theatre and public library" while tall chimney stacks proclaim it the seat of numerous industries — woollen, coach, butter and cheese factories, and a brewery". Milton, a comparable secondary centre in Otago, supported potteries, lime kilns, flour and oatmeal mills. Even Picton, "a very small place" in the mid 1880s, boasted "five hotels ... its own newspaper, and ... a full quota of churches, besides telegraph office, court-house and hospital" and was connected by rail to Blenheim.

Though industries flourished in some of these secondary centres, most industry was concentrated in the four main centres. Many city dwellers earned their living handling the products of farmers. But manufacturing industries provided a living for many other city dwellers, although in 1885 workers in secondary industries were only three per cent of the total population.

Dunedin owed an early start as an industrial centre to the Otago gold rushes. By the 1880s it had foundries and an engineering works at which iron steamships and dredges were being built. Nearby at Mosgiel, woollen mills, the first in the country, were employing 400 hands in the mid 1880s. Another mill at Roslyn employed 450. A mammoth clothing factory manufactured goods for a nationwide chain. "The great smoke stacks which may be seen rising in various parts of the city are monster signal-posts reared by industrial energy which ... excite in the mind of the beholder visions of a future Birmingham or Sheffield . . arising on a site where forty years ago stood the primeval forest' wrote an observer impressed by Dunedin's industrial muscle.

Christchurch had a similar variety of industries — flourmills, implement manufactories, brick, carpet and carriage foundries, brass and copper works, breweries, potteries, pickle, sauce and jam works, fellmongeries, tanneries and biscuit factories. A Christchurch engineering works turned out the first locomotives manufactured in New Zealand. Nearby at Kaiapoi were a woollen mill and glass works. Wellington and Auckland were not far behind these South Island centres in the variety and size of their factories.

The power for New Zealand industry came at first from wind and from water. Water-power remained important for many years, the simple waterwheel giving way to the high-pressure pelton wheel, then to the turbine. But by the mid 1880s steam was driving most of the wheels of New Zealand industry.

Marked improvements in transportation within and between the country's cities accompanied their growth. The horse remained pre-eminent, ridden or drawing carts, waggons and coaches and the first trams. But gradually horses faced increasing competition for land travel from steam-driven trains and trams (and from bicycles). By the mid 1880s Auckland had a tramway running from the Queen Street Wharf to Epsom and Ponsonby. In Wellington trams were running between the Railway Station and Newtown and in Christchurch from Sydenham to Papanui and east to the Heathcote Bridge. Cable cars were carrying passengers up Dunedin's steeper streets.

Railways helped to knit the separated settlements together. The line between Lyttelton and Bluff was completed in 1879. Wellington was linked by rail to New Plymouth in 1886 and to Napier in 1891. The North Island Main Trunk was surveyed in the 1880s, but not finished until twenty years later. In the meantime, travellers from Wellington to Auckland customarily took the train to New Plymouth and then a steamer to Onehunga. Telegraph lines carried messages between the centres. The first cable under Cook Strait was laid in 1866. (Only fourteen years earlier, in 1852, news from Auckland was a month old by the time it reached Christchurch).

Much transportation between different parts of New Zealand continued, throughout the nineteenth century, to be by sea, as did all transportation between New Zealand and the rest of the world. Ports developed along with the cities they served. Substantial harbour works were put in train and coastal defences built during the Russian scares of the 1880s. Lighthouses made navigation around New Zealand's wild coasts less hazardous. The first was built in 1859 on Pencarrow Head at the entrance to Wellington Harbour. A few more followed in the 1860s, then many more in the 1870s and 1880s.

But there was a dark side to this story of urban progress and development in nineteenth century New Zealand. In the late 1870s and 1880s the situation of the urban working classes deteriorated as New Zealand struggled through the long depression which followed the Vogel boom. In the late 1870s unemployment began to become a serious problem and local bodies had to begin providing relief work. Numbers of New Zealanders came to depend for their welfare on such institutions as refuges for homeless women and homes for destitute men and for the elderly poor.

During the Vogel boom, New Zealand had been ''an El Dorado for the industrious working man'' but the urban working classes suffered severely in the long depression of the 1880s, working often for low wages in poor conditions. Towards the end of the 1880s, the plight of one group of urban workers became particularly acute. These were the women who worked in the clothing trade — in small workshops or in their homes. 'Sweating' in Dunedin and Christchurch became such a scandal that, prompted in part by a Presbyterian minister delivering a thundering sermon on ''the Sin of Cheapness'', the Government set up a Royal Commission to investigate the plight of these women.

During these times of distress for the urban poor and working classes, trade unions first emerged as a force in New Zealand life. Immigrants of the 1870s brought to New Zealand British trade union and friendly society traditions. The new unions were strongest in the transport and coalmining industries. The rise of unions was deplored by the upper classes, but the new organisations were supported enthusiastically by the workers themselves. ''The union has been a great boon to us. I would not for anything wish it was dissolved'' a shirt-finisher told the Sweating Commission in 1890.

Economic hardship and unemployment helped to swell the ranks of the larrikins who were responsible for the vandalism, incendiarism and petty crime that beset New Zealand cities in the 1870s and 1880s. They probably also played their part in causing widespread public drunkenness. Butler had noticed in the 1860s ''a far greater tendency towards drink'' in New Zealand than in England, and by the 1880s many were observing that a propensity for drink among both sexes was strongly developed in New Zealand. The abuse of alcohol was sufficiently widespread to make the temperance and prohibition causes among the strongest movements in late nineteenth century New Zealand.

Sometimes urban disorder in late nineteenth century New Zealand was social rather than individual. In 1879 in Christchurch a procession of Orangemen degenerated into an attack on Irish immigrants and other mobs found other occasions or reasons for near-riotous behaviour in New Zealand cities in the late 1870s and 1880s. As New Zealand's cities grew in size and became more imposing architecturally they did not necessarily become more civilised orderly places, than the tiny wooden townships of thirty of forty years earlier. They were certainly no calmer than New Zealand cities today.

By the end of the nineteenth century, although New Zealand was a predominantly farming country, many New Zealanders were living close-packed on urban streets (Page 50 Inset).
Until an Education Act was passed in the 1870s, New Zealand children were not particularly well educated. Church-run schools, like the Bishop's School, Nelson, (Above & Left) made up some of the deficiencies in the public education systems of the Provinces.

153

In the 1870s, both Dunedin and Christchurch graduated to the status of university cities. Otago University's fine stone buildings (Opp.) were built in the late 1870s.

Gentlemen's Clubs, another hallmark of 'real' cities in the nineteenth century, were set up in all the main centres. The Christchurch Club, (Left) the social headquarters of Christchurch's runholder-merchant elite, was built in 1861. In Auckland, the Northern Club (Below) opened the doors of its plastered brick building in the late 1860s.

THE NORTHERN CLUB
1869

One of the pleasures of life in nineteenth century Christchurch was boating on the Avon River in a boat hired from one of the many boatsheds (Right) on the river's banks.
Rowing was also a popular competitive sport in nineteenth century New Zealand. The Star Rowing Club, established in 1856, moved into new boatsheds on the Wellington waterfront (Above) in 1885.

Only 20 or 30 years after settlement began in earnest, New Zealand's towns and cities were thriving, if not yet sophisticated. Their shops (Left & Bottom) stocked all manner of imported and domestic goods. There were barbers' shops (Below) to which gentlemen could repair for their daily shave.

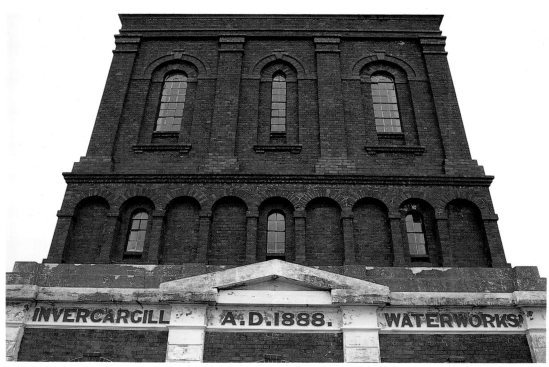

INVERCARGILL A.D. 1888. WATERWORKS

Gradually the towns and cities acquired urban amenities and services which made them pleasanter, and safer, places to live. In towns built largely of wood, fire stations (Left) were among the important services provided early on by local governments. In the late 1880s, Invercargill, built on low-lying, flat ground, constructed a high brick water tower (Above) to provide itself with high-pressure water, for fighting fires and to supply homes and industries.

161

Banks were among the first commercial buildings to give New Zealand towns a permanent, established air. Their imposing architecture was intended to impress customers with the bank's solidity and reliability. The Australia and New Zealand Bank opened its grand Dunedin premises (Above Right) in 1874. Public buildings soon matched the banks and other business premises. When Christchurch's Post Office (Above) opened in 1879 it housed a number of other government departments besides the Post Office in accustomed splendour.

In the cities, too, were built large and increasingly grand hotels (Top & Right) which provided accommodation for travellers passing through or for country folk visiting town.

The pride of Victorian New Zealanders in the new towns they were creating was evident in the ways in which they decorated and embellished their buildings and their cities.

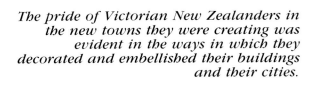

165

Most of the earliest churches and other ecclesiastical buildings
in New Zealand towns were modest wooden structures. In
Auckland, St Stephen's Chapel (Above) was built in 1856 and
Bishopscourt, residence of Bishop Selwyn, (Right)
in the early 1860s.

As the towns grew, many congregations aspired to build larger
churches of brick or stone, different denominations sometimes
vying with each other to build the most impressive buildings.
Dunedin's First Church (Opp. Bottom Right), in Presbyterian
Otago, was built in 1868-73 in the Gothic style most thought
proper for churches. Dunedin's Roman Catholic Cathedral
(Opp. Top) St Joseph's, 1886.

The buildings of Roman Catholic institutions, like St Dominic's
Priory in Dunedin, built of concrete in 1877, (Opp. Bottom
Left) were among the largest buildings in many cities and
country towns. A truly urban building, St Dominic's sits hard
up against a street on its tight site.

Many visitors to New Zealand were surprised to find even the wealthy who lived in the cities occupying houses built of wood. They were often large, rambling houses, like Alberton in Auckland, (Pgs 168-9 and Opp.) added to over the years as their owners amassed more money and acquired more children. Alberton's owner, Allan Kerr Taylor, had been born in India and when the house was enlarged in 1872, verandahs, balconies and towers faintly Indian in style were added (Right), giving the front of the house an exotic air. Alberton was a centre of Auckland's social life in the 1870s and 1880s, the scene of balls, entertainments, dinner parties and 'at homes' in the spacious rooms downstairs (Two Below). The family's bedrooms upstairs (Right)were more intimate but still rather grand.

While the adults at least of upper class families lived in style and comfort, the servants had to be content with small attic bedrooms (Opp. Top Right). A good part of the servants' working lives were spent in the kitchen (Right) preparing meals on the coal range (Above) or in the wash-house (Opp. Top Left) washing by hand the family's personal laundry and linen.

When the families of even
the rich were large, the
children did not enjoy
much more space or
comfort than the servants.
Alfred Buckland, the owner
of Auckland's Highwic, had
21 children and the
Buckland boys, when
young, slept crowded in an
upstairs dormitory tucked
under the roof.
(Pg 174-175)

The smaller houses of the middle and working classes were, even more commonly than the houses of the rich, built of wood. A typical worker's cottage (Above Right) might have just two rooms each side of a short central hall, with the kitchen in a lean-to at the back. Some had tiny attic rooms while many sported verandahs (Above).
On Wellington's steep hills, land suitable for building was scarce and small wooden houses were tucked on to odd, angular sites (Above Left). Most nineteenth century New Zealanders, even townsfolk, lived in detached wooden houses on their own sections. But in a few cities, notably Dunedin, terrace houses were built of brick or stone (Right).

Most nineteenth century New Zealand homes were built of wood, but this did not prevent those who could afford to from building impressively grand dwellings. In 1854 and 1861 two wealthy Nelson merchants built, in two stages, a veritable castle of wood, with towers and turrets (Top Right). But good building stone was to be found in many localities and sometimes used for houses, as it was for Isel House (Right) at Stoke, near Nelson.
Wooden fretwork was the most common form of decoration on nineteenth century New Zealand houses, but cast iron (Top) was also popular. Most urban New Zealanders enjoyed door-to-door postal deliveries (Above) while in the country most settlers had to collect their mail from the nearest post office.

The cities supported sizeable and reasonably well-off professional and commercial classes whose homes were bigger than those of most New Zealand town-dwellers. For the house of the early clergyman and schoolmaster, John Kinder (Below Left) built in Parnell, Auckland, in 1856-57, a dark local stone was used. For a grand townhouse on Dunedin's Royal Terrace (Left) the builder used double brick which was then plastered over. In the 1890s, the house became the home of the wealthy founder of a biscuit and chocolate manufacturing firm.

It was not just the rich who could look forward to being well-housed. A labourer who had arrived in Nelson in 1842 had, by about 1860, managed to accumulate enough money to build what was, though a simple cottage in form with verandah, dormers and decorated bargeboards, still a good, solid dwelling for its time (Below) with thick walls of cob.

*Nelson's Melrose (Above) is a magnificent mansion built solidly
of wood, fashioned to give the impression of the grandeur and
permanence of stone, with a slate roof. It was built probably in
1876 by a leading merchant who had prospered as the town of
Nelson grew.*
*Highwic (Top & Left) in Auckland, the home of the prosperous
Auckland businessman, Alfred Buckland, was built in the
popular domestic Gothic style. Through additions and
alterations, Buckland turned the originally modest house into
one befitting his wealth and status in early Auckland.*

The urban elite which lived in large houses like Highwic maintained a standard of living equal to that of the great station owners, filling their houses with imported furniture and household goods, entertaining in style and enjoying luxury in their private lives (Below & Left).

Some members of the urban upper classes built their grand houses on rural sites on the outskirts of the cities. William Larnach, who made his fortune in banking and the timber and hardware trades, chose a commanding hill-top site on the Otago Peninsula for his 'castle' (Right and Far Right). Construction of the mansion started in 1871, but the ballroom, the last major addition, was not completed until 1887. Local craftsmen were kept supplied with imported and the very best domestic materials to fashion an interior with stone and wood work which made it one of the most lavish in New Zealand (Below Right). Three men spent six and a half years carving the ornate ceiling of the entrance hall (Below)

187

Though nineteenth century New Zealand was primarily a farming country, by the end of the century it was also the home of many flourishing, large-scale industries. In 1884, the first Portland cement works in the Southern Hemisphere (Previous Page) were erected at Warkworth, north of Auckland.

Mining, a major New Zealand industry throughout the nineteenth century, began in the earliest days of European settlement. Copper was being mined on Kawau Island (Opp. top) in the early 1840s.

Burnt lime was needed in large quantities for the mortar which held together buildings of brick and stone. The kilns in which the limestone was burned were themselves built solidly of brick or stone. The circular kiln at Sandymount (Opp. Bottom) on the Otago Peninsula was lit for the first time in 1865.

Flour mills, usually powered by water, were built in many country areas to grind locally grown wheat. In timberless Central Otago flour mills, like the mill erected near Oturehua in 1884 (Above), were built solidly of stone. Most New Zealand cities, and many smaller towns, had their own breweries, supplying the wants of local people. The malthouse at Dunedin's Union Brewery (Opp. Centre) was built in the 1880s.

Large crops of wheat were grown in Canterbury and Otago in the nineteenth century. Some of the wheat provided the basis for a flourishing flour milling industry. A four-storey mill was built of local limestone at Maheno in 1866 (Left & Below). The mill was driven by an overshot waterwheel to which water was led in a race from the Kakanui River. In later years a turbine replaced the waterwheel and rollers were installed in place of the original millstones.
The introduction of trams revolutionised transportation within New Zealand's cities, fostering a sprawl of suburbs before the nineteenth century was out. The trams were first horse-drawn, then steam driven and finally, from about the turn of the century, powered by electricity (Following Page).

Trains did for transportation between towns and cities what trams did for transportation within them, making it far easier for ordinary folk to move about. Steam trains needed constant supplies of water for their boilers. Windmills (Above) were built to pump water into trackside tanks to replenish the locomotives.

Long after the first trains were running on New Zealand railway lines, horsedrawn coaches (Left) which had first provided long-distance overland transportation when European settlement began, were still maintaining links on many routes between towns and cities not served by trains.

Much travel around New Zealand in the nineteenth century was made not by land but by sea. Coastal vessels linked major and secondary ports and often provided quicker, more comfortable transportation than was available by land. Lighthouses were built around New Zealand's long coastline to ensure the safety of coastal and overseas shipping. The wooden lighthouse on the North Head of the Kaipara Harbour (Above Left), once a busy timber port, was built in 1884.

A steam train first carried passengers on a New Zealand line in 1863. For the rest of the century steam locomotives (Below) had only horses as rivals for importance in pulling New Zealanders and their goods around the country. The important role that rail transport played in nineteenth and early twentieth century New Zealand life was obvious in the number and size of the country's railway stations. None were grander than Dunedin's magnificent stone station (Opp. Left) opened in 1907. Across its mosaic tile floor (Left) trod the feet of thousands of travellers, commuters taking local trains and long-distance travellers heading north to Christchurch or south to Invercargill on the main trunk line express.

The stations of smaller towns along the lines were generally built of wood and iron, with platform canopies to protect the waiting travellers (Opp. Below Right).

A New Nation

"A daring little land of successful big experiments."
Outlook Magazine 1910

The General Election of 1890, one of the turning points in New Zealand's history, was fought as a battle "between the champions of the people and the champions of privilege". The victorious Liberal Party went to the electorate promising efforts to put the small man on the land by busting up the big estates, a broad programme of social reform, and a place in the political system for trade unions. The support of small farmers (and or rural workers who aspired to become farmers) and of urban workers put the Liberals in power. In later years farmers and urban workers were to fall apart politically and support opposing parties — the Reform and later National Parties winning the allegiance of the farmers and the Labour Party that of the urban workers. But until 1912 the Liberals managed to hold their broad coalition together and to stay in power.

Immediately after its 1890 election victory, the Liberal Party was impeded in putting its programme into effect by a constitutional tussle over the place of the Upper House (now abolished) in the political system. By 1893 the Liberals had successfully asserted the pre-eminence of the Lower House. This paved the way for a burst of legislation which transformed New Zealand life. It was, in its way, a bloodless social revolution. The New Zealand which this legislation brought into being, is recognisably the New Zealand of today. The Liberal 'revolution' was the last stage in the birth of a distinctively New Zealand nation. The legislation was not without precedent. George Grey had come to power in 1878 on a platform of creating a landowning democracy of small farmers, but he fell from power after a short term in office with little achieved. Some of the 'conservative' ministries of the 1880s had attempted to implement some progressive reforms, but with scant success. What the Liberals did was finally to force these and other reforms through.

Land policy was at the heart of the Liberal programme. The Liberal Minister of Lands, John McKenzie, had risen himself from poor shepherd to landowner. He was the sworn enemy of land monopolists and the champion of small holders. A land tax and an act allowing the Government to repurchase large estates set the stage for the breaking up of many of the estates into smaller farms and runs. Repurchase of the Cheviot Estate in North Canterbury in 1892 under the land tax legislation was hailed as an important first step in putting land into the hands of working farmers. Some estate owners, seeing the writing on the wall, subdivided their estates without waiting for the Government to repurchase them. In 1894 the Advances to Settlers Act provided those who took up the newly subdivided land with the cheap loans they needed to establish themselves as farmers. In the period up to 1914 the land in large holdings shrank dramatically and the number of small farmers increased. They prospered supplying butter, cheese and meat to the English market, opened up to them by refrigeration.

For urban workers, the Industrial Conciliation and Arbitration Act of 1894 set up a machinery to settle industrial disputes which gave the unions a place they were content to occupy for several years. A Factory Act regulated hours and conditions of work and ended the worst exploitation of workers. On the social front, an Old Age Pensions Act, passed in 1898, was New Zealand's first major piece of welfare legislation. Women were given the vote in 1893. (New Zealand was the first country in the world to introduce women's suffrage).

Although the changes were sweeping, and advanced in their time, the Liberals passed their legislation in a pragmatic, untheoretical spirit. "Socialism without doctrine" was how a French observer described it. Few New Zealanders of the day had any fear of the State taking the active role given to it by the Liberal legislation. Atkinson, a 'conservative' Premier of the 1880s, voiced the prevailing New Zealand attitude: "What is the meaning of a State but that we all band together to do certain things and to promote certain ends that we desire". So by the end of the nineteenth century New Zealanders, lacking the fear of the State prevalent in older, larger societies in which there were greater disparities of wealth and privilege, had happily accepted the State running railways, the telegraph system, the post office, an insurance office, a savings bank, a public trust office. The State was educating most New Zealand children, providing for the needy in their old age, helping farmers onto the land, intervening in industrial disputes, protecting workers against exploitation... The Liberal legislation of the 1890s did not initiate this entrusting of many functions to the State, but it carried it further than it had been taken before and made it, irrevocably, a distinctive feature of New Zealand life long before the first Labour Government's legislation in the 1930s.

The Liberal legislation earned New Zealand an extraordinary, world-wide reputation. A 1901 newspaper editorial declared complacently that New Zealand was "the most democratic community in the English speaking world...the most advanced and probably the most intelligent Democracy of the age". It was because New Zealanders had been told, repeatedly, that their country was "in the van of civilisation", "a daring little land of successful big experiments", "the birthplace of the twentieth century", that they formed such a high opinion of their country. There was a certain amount of humbug in the way New Zealanders repeated such phrases. The Premier, Richard John Seddon, was admonished in Parliament on his return from Britain in 1897: "You must not think New Zealand is the Universe". But being held up as an example to the world, fed the new national self confidence that was evident in New Zealand at the turn of the century.

The Liberal Party had entered office under the leadership of John Ballance. When Ballance died in 1893, the leadership was taken over by Seddon, who dominated the country until his own death in 1906. He was a new type of political leader in New Zealand: bluff, hearty, direct, popular. The 'gentlemen politicians' of earlier decades were eclipsed. From Seddon's time until today successful New Zealand leaders have all been men of the people. Although he was born in Lancashire, Seddon, who cut his political teeth on the West Coast of the South Island, could only have been a New Zealander. His colonial character grated somewhat on the educated, cultured British Socialist, Beatrice Webb. She found him "incurably rough in manner", "intensely vulgar", but also "shrewd, quick, genial". The differences between Seddon and Webb are indicative of the extent to which a distinct colonial, New Zealand character had been formed by the end of the nineteenth century.

A distinct character is one of the marks of nationhood and the emergence of such a character had been noticed very early in New Zealand's colonial days. Godley, the Canterbury Association's agent, had remarked in 1852 that after a young man had spent a few years in a new country "a new set of habits have been generated, not necessarily worse habits, but different ones which make the thought of a permanent residence in an old

New Zealand.

P. 07/1883
with 1907/2256

COLONIAL SECRETARY.

190 7.

Received: 29. 10

From Secretary of State for Colonies.
London.

Subject: Forwdg: (1) Copies of O/C approving the issue of a Proclamation changing designation of N.Z. to "Dominion of N.Z." and (2) Copies of the Royal Proclamation.

12. 9. , 190 7.

(6,000/9/1906—8085)

MEMORANDA.

Recommended that copy of despatch and enclosures be presented to both Houses of the General Assembly by command
Hugh Wallen[?]
29.10.07.

or messages?

Appd
[signature]
29.10.07

Make two typewritten copies of despatch and make up as a Parl. paper. advising the Esley to command presentation.
[initials] 30/10/07

(made up as a Parl. Paper) made & advice to Governor prepared
30.10.07

country distasteful to him". Samuel Butler in the 1860s observed that "there is much nonsense in the old country from which people here are free. There is little conventionalism, little formality and much liberality of sentiment; very little sectarianism, and, as a general rule, a healthy, sensible tone in conversation".

Both Butler and Godley returned to 'the old country' but most who came stayed to take part in the fraternising of different ranks which left New Zealand society, to English eyes, "in a curious state of muddle". A levelling up and down and a marked social fluidity became characteristic of New Zealand life from early colonial days. "A man may be managing a bank on your forming his acquaintance" wrote one observer "and you are somewhat amazed to discover at one period of his previous history he had been a bullock-driver carting goods to the diggings". Colonials were found to have a remarkable "versatility of disposition", a "knack of turning to anything". The breaking down of social distinctions and easy assumption of different roles by people of all social classes was partly the result of there being so few people. "Classes are to mix more here" one new colonist wrote home in 1851 "or there would be no society at all". In a relatively empty land people tended also to be on the move more than in England; driven by "a roving disposition" colonists were "always ready to move elsewhere should things appear brighter or more lucrative in another part". (The disillusioned colonist who made this observation thought it a fault that there was in New Zealand "no attachment to place, loyalty, or friends as in England").

The circumstances of colonial life required the upper classes in particular to change and adapt. There was no place for standing on airs or for upper class indolence in the new country. In his farewell speech to the Canterbury colonists, just two years after the settlement had been founded, Godley remarked that "in new countries every man must do something, and every man finds something to do. I have seen here clergymen ploughing, and barristers digging, and officers of the army and navy 'riding in' stock, and no-one thought the worse of them". Labour was dear, obliging people "to do things for themselves which, had they remained in the country whence they came, they would never have thought of attempting". Any appearance of "uppishness" was quickly resented. A workman told by a new arrival from England that he had no right to be on a certain property retorted "Oh we make rights for ourselves in this country". People of the middle and upper classes noticed a marked lack of deference among the lower orders. "You and your men" Butler advised prospective runholders "will have to be on a rather different footing from that on which you stood in England". The men would be respectful and civil, said Butler, but there would be "a slight but quite unobjectionable difference in their manner towards you". A clergyman on the West Coast in the 1860s observed that the New Zealand gold digger had "a way of treating you on the equal standing of your manhood, as if class distinctions did not exist". In Dunedin it was noticed that "on calling at a house there is sometimes a difficulty in knowing whether it is a housemaid or a member of the family who opens the door for you, caps and such like minor distinctions . . . being utterly abolished in this land of freedom". Gradually through the nineteenth century these and other distinctive characteristics became impressed on those who stayed long or, increasingly, grew up in New Zealand. In the 1870s a writer noted that "colonial youth are always hearing their elders' far-off native land, spoken of by those around them with feelings of affection and thus ideas are generated that in New Zealand there is not much to be proud of". But, the writer went on, "as the proportion of native-born population to immigrants increases, a national feeling will arise". New Zealand was likely in time, he concluded, to produce "a truly patriotic, if not a boasting people". By Seddon's time New

Zealanders, not least Seddon himself, were marked by such a boasting patriotism. And by Seddon's time, native-born children outnumbered their immigrant parents. Most of the New Zealand born, as well as many of the immigrants, like Seddon, had characters and personalities quite unlike those of their English counterparts. (In one other demographic way New Zealand assumed, in the Seddon era a characteristic it still has. By 1901, the North Island had overtaken the South in population. The completion of the North Island Main Trunk Railway in 1908 can be taken as symbolic of the North Island's rise to dominance).

There were many signs around the turn of the century of a new, truly patriotic spirit, based on an awareness that New Zealanders had gone their own way. When a Parliamentary committee recommended, in 1899, that a new Chief Librarian be selected in England, the House of Representatives indignantly and decisively carried an amendment that attempts to be made first to secure a librarian in New Zealand. In 1902 New Zealand adopted its own national flag, the flag that still flies today. At the same time, New Zealand decided not to join the new Australian federation. The commission set up to examine the possibility of New Zealand's joining with the Australian states in the new federation decided that "the stretch of some 1200 miles of sea between Australia and New Zealand is a weighty argument against New Zealand joining the Commonwealth". The commission argued that "New Zealand as a colony can herself supply all that can be required to support and maintain within her boundaries, a population which might at no distant date be worthily styled a nation".

In 1907 New Zealand decided that, even if it were not yet a nation, it had outgrown being a colony. In that year New Zealand was proclaimed a Dominion and its colonial period came formally to an end. To one M.P., New Zealand's assumption of Dominion Status suggested "a very small man wearing a very large hat". An American observer, present when the proclamation was read to a crowd of several thousand from the steps of Parliament Building, noted that "there was no enthusiasm; a few cheers fell stillborn and the crowd of merely curious onlookers melted away in silence". But an American was not perhaps the best person to judge the mood of a typically undemonstrative New Zealand crowd and Sir Joseph Ward, the Prime Minister of the day, was confident that the change demonstrated that the country had outgrown the colonial stage and was asserting its status in the eyes of the world.

At the beginning of the twentieth century New Zealand still lacked some of the attributes of nationhood. The signs of a truly New Zealand literature were there in the work of poets like Jessie Mackay and William Pember Reeves, but to a large extent New Zealand was still, intellectually and culturally, as B.E. Baughan described it in 1908, "a country to come". Many of New Zealand's most gifted young in the early twentieth century — the writer Katherine Mansfield and the painter Frances Hodgkins among them — had to leave New Zealand to flourish as artists.

At the beginning of the twentieth century, too, New Zealand was extravagantly — but not slavishly — loyal to the British Empire. The ties linking New Zealand to Great Britain were many. They included those of sentiment — "the traditions of race and origin" — and of strategy — New Zealand enjoyed the protection of the world's strongest navy. Economically, Britain provided New Zealand with loans to finance further development and with a market for farm products. But belonging to the Empire was not, in the minds of New Zealanders of the day, incompatible with national spirit and independence. For it was seen as an empire of equals, a mutually beneficial partnership of independent, self-governing States. Britain had not made any serious attempt to interfere with the right of New Zealanders to govern themselves since the 1850s. New Zealand did not have to break its ties to Britain to preserve its "free constitution" and "right of self-government". Membership of the Empire gave New Zealand security and a standing in the world it would not otherwise have enjoyed, supporting rather than undermining New Zealanders' self-confidence in their emerging nationhood.

In defence, membership of the Empire spared New Zealand having to acquire its own navy to defend its interests because the British Navy seemed a sure defence against any threat. But as one aspect of a growing sense of its own standing and importance, New Zealand took on its own shoulders a share of the cost of maintaining the Royal Navy and sent troops to South Africa to fight for the British in the Boer War.

But even in this area of defence there were occasional calls for New Zealand to become truly independent. When a bill which provided for New Zealand to contribute £100,000 a year for ten years towards maintaining the Royal Navy was being debated in Parliament, one member demanded to know: "Are we everlastingly to go crying to our mother for everything that we desire? Are we never to be grown up? Are we always to be children depending upon our mother for sustenance and support?" When America's Great White Fleet visited Auckland in 1908 there were glimmerings of a perception that New Zealand's interests might some day not be protected by Britain and that America would be a more important guardian or ally. But for the most part at the beginning of the twentieth century New Zealanders were content to enjoy the protection of the British Navy, without any feeling that this made New Zealand in any significant way less of a free nation itself. Although no conflict of loyalties was felt by most, there were hints that if such a conflict ever arose, loyalty to New Zealand would come ahead of loyalty to the Empire, however beneficial membership of the Empire was. An M.P., proud to have been "born under the Southern Cross", declared in 1897 that he was "a New Zealand colonist first, and a native of the British Empire afterwards".

In one other important way, New Zealand at the beginning of the twentieth century was already far along the way of becoming the nation it is today. In the later nineteenth century, the Maori people, with whom New Zealand's story began, were squeezed out into the margins of New Zealand society and history. Demoralised by the continuing loss of their land, still prey to diseases against which they lacked effective immunity, their numbers fell steadily. They looked to many at the century's end like the remnant of a dying race, their only place being to provide a touch of native colour to such occasions as the great exhibition held in Christchurch in 1906-1907. But the 1901 census recorded a slight increase in Maori numbers from the 1896 low of 42,000. The Liberals, in their consuming passion to get the small farmer on the land, accelerated the passing of land from Maori into European hands, but made some effort to extend schooling, health services and other welfare support into Maori communities. More importantly, from within Maori society itself a new leadership emerged. Although separated to some extent from the tribal, rural ways in which most Maori still lived, the leaders of this Maori renaissance — Aspirana Ngata, Maui Pomare and Peter Buck — served notice on European New Zealand that the Maori people and Maori society would survive. Ngata entered Parliament in 1905 and remained an M.P. for many years. Buck and Pomare combined political with medical careers and Buck went on to a further career as an anthropologist. After the first decade of the twentieth century, little more was heard of the Maori as a dying race. There was no longer any doubt that in the future of New Zealand both races would have to have a part.

The first of the three buildings which make up today's Parliament Buildings in Wellington, the General Assembly Library (Pg 202 Inset) was built in a confident Gothic style at the very end of the nineteenth century. In 1907 New Zealand discarded the title 'Colony', so symbolically shedding its status of subservience to Great Britain. A British Order in Council (Page 203) paved the way for a Proclamation which declared that New Zealand was now a Dominion.

In September 1907 New Zealand shrugged off the title 'Colony' and emerged as a 'Dominion'. A large crowd gathered in Wellington to hear the Prime Minister, Sir Joseph Ward, read the proclamation declaring New Zealand a Dominion from the steps of Parliament. Their numbers suggested that many New Zealanders of the day realised that it marked an important step along the path to nationhood for a country of, by then, almost a million people.

The King Proclaims New Zealand a Dominion: Sir Joseph Ward, Premier, Reading the Proclamation from the Steps of Parliament House, Wellington, September 26th, 1907.

Key to location of photographs